Pr

"You can read lo … tell a story. Unlike them, *Story Power* … art, with twenty-one diverse voices and fascinating tales that entertain as you learn how to create and craft personal stories of all types. Seasoned storyteller Kate Farrell offers up her proven, seven-step approach along with engaging prompts and exercises and creates a storytelling guide for everyone with a story they want to tell—and tell well."

—**Nina Amir**, author coach, Certified High Performance Coach, bestselling author of *How to Blog a Book, The Author Training Manual, and Creative Visualization for Writers*

"This master storyteller has gifted those of us who love the power of story with a seven-step process for crafting them or (as the author might say) seven steps to spinning the straw of our stories into gold. I warmly invite you into these sage, inspiring pages that are abundantly filled not only with Kate Farrell's multilayered wisdom, but also accompanied by the diverse voices and styles of many other award-winning storytellers. This is a vibrant and enlightening new book by a master storyteller."

—**Mary Jo Doig**, author of *Patchwork: A Memoir of Love and Loss*, Story Circle Network board member, chair of Circles Work Group, and a Story Circle book reviewer

"From speeches to dinnertime stories to toasts at weddings, our culture is awash with storytelling—and here at last is a guide to help any anyone craft a better story. *Story Power* explores what makes a memorable story, offers techniques from a variety of writers and tellers, and provides tips to overcome common challenges for both practiced and impromptu storytelling. Written in a clear, compelling style, this guide is as engaging as a good story itself."

—**Martha Conway**, author of *The Underground River* (*New York Times* Book Review Editor's Choice)

"A great book for writers! Are you ready to become adept at telling (not writing) your story? As an author, there will be innumerable times when you will need to pitch the premise of your book, describe how you got into the writing business, or provide your brief biography. *Story Power* will help you identify the stories that will resonate with others, teach you powerful oral and written storytelling techniques, and help you discover your storytelling style and voice.

"*Story Power* fills a unique place on an author's bookshelf—it is a tool for furthering your career, a workbook to distill your memories and experiences into useful anecdotes, and a guide to finding a new voice through the oral tradition of storytelling."

—**Taryn Edwards**, historian, librarian, manager of writers' activities at the Mechanics' Institute of San Francisco

"In this fascinating compendium, Kate Farrell goes to the heart of one of the most ancient traditions on earth: storytelling. What is most important is that she brings the tradition up to date and brings us along with her. You will read its pages for the insightful words of published writers and examples of their storytelling, a joy in themselves, but you will also read it to learn how to bring your own stories to life on the page, on the stage, around a campfire, or at a dinner table. *Story Power* is both a toolbox and a treasure chest. You will go back to it many times."

—Award-winning journalist **Mary Jo McConahay**, author of *The Tango War: The Struggle for the Hearts, Minds and Riches of Latin America During World War II*

"Stories define us, give us identity, and shape us into who we are and will become. Threads of our stories take us into the unknown caverns of the self where new gold may be found—the treasures of our truths that can set us free. In this storytelling guide, you will be inspired to consider the stories that have shaped you and those you can share. Having witnesses to our lives and an audience are important parts of creating wholeness. *Story Power* offers the inspiration and the clues about how to incorporate stories and storytelling into the fabric of your life."

—**Linda Joy Myers**, founder of the National Association of Memoir Writers, author of *Don't Call Me Mother* and *Song of the Plains*

"If you're looking for a guide to the art of storytelling, look no further than Kate Farrell's *Story Power*. Using examples and advice contributed by over twenty successful writers, Farrell shows us how and why they succeed at transforming life events into distilled, impactful stories. Each chapter provides tips, examples, prompts, and exercises to help you select significant events from your own life—early childhood to adult life, family secrets to family lore—and craft them into compelling narratives. *Story Power* dives into the age-old reasons for oral storytelling: self-discovery, connection, inspiration, influence, and passing on family traditions. Everyone tells stories—*Story Power* will help you craft and deliver yours with powerful results."

—**Amber Lea Starfire**, editor, writing coach, and author of *Not the Mother I Remember* and *Accidental Jesus Freak—One Woman's Journey from Fundamentalism to Freedom*

"The best thing about sharing stories from your life is that you are the author. If only you could craft your adventures, anecdotes, and memories into a memorable art form—you can with the tips and ideas offered in Story Power! Kate Farrell holds your hand, offering guidance and encouraging you to develop your own stories and tell them anywhere and everywhere, from entertaining family and friends to storytelling performances. Story Power shows how crafting and telling stories is a winning combination."

—**Ruth Stotter**, former director of the Dominican University Certificate-in-Storytelling program, a Fulbright scholar, and recipient of the Lifetime Oracle Achievement Award from the National Association of Storytellers.

"In Story Power, author Kate Farrell answers that fraught question, "Do I have a story to tell?" with a resounding 'Yes!' Mining her own experiences, Farrell offers small narrative gems alongside craft tips, commentary, and writing samples from an impressive list of acclaimed authors. Learn travel writing from Lisa Alpine, for example, or keys to crafting adventure stories from Mary Mackey, or personal branding from Marissa Moss. In this social media era of instant impulse, Story Power teaches us to slow down and to reflect upon, frame, and transform the raw material of experience into stories worth sharing. Engaging and accessible, Story Power will help you jump-start and sustain your writing practice; Story Power is a gift to writing teachers and writers at all stages of their careers."

—**Mary Volmer**, author of Reliance, Illinois and professor of English and Collegiate Seminar at Saint Mary's College, California

STORY
POWER

STORY POWER

SECRETS TO CREATING, CRAFTING, AND TELLING MEMORABLE STORIES

KATE FARRELL

CORAL GABLES

Cover Design: Jayoung Hong
illustration: WinWin artlab/ Shutterstock
Layout & Design: Jayoung Hong

For permission requests, please contact the publisher at:
Mango Publishing Group
2850 S Douglas Road, 2nd Floor
Coral Gables, FL 33134 USA
info@mango.bz

For special orders, quantity sales, course adoptions and corporate sales, please email the publisher at sales@mango.bz. For trade and wholesale sales, please contact Ingram Publisher Services at customer.service@ingramcontent.com or +1.800.509.4887.

Story Power: Secrets to Creating, Crafting, and Telling Memorable Stories

Library of Congress Cataloging-in-Publication number: 2020933899
ISBN: (p) 978-1-64250-197-1 (e) 978-1-64250-198-8
BISAC category code LAN005060, LANGUAGE ARTS & DISCIPLINES / Writing / Nonfiction (incl. Memoirs)

Printed in the United States of America

To your powerful stories!

Table of Contents

Foreword

As women, we have always found ourselves in story.

From the beginning of human existence, while we planted
and harvested and prepared food, spun thread and wove
cloth, tended our babies and cared for our elderly parents, we
told one another the stories of our lives and the lives of our
grandmothers and mothers and daughters and granddaughters.
Our shared stories became a many-voiced chorus singing the
same song: the story-song of women at work and women at
play, women loving and living, women birthing, women dying.
Those stories were full of pain because human lives have always
been like that. They were full of joy because lives are like that,
too. Pain and joy were woven like golden threads through the
full, rich, round stories of women's lives, passed from mother to
daughter to granddaughter through the generations so that the
experiences of women would not be forgotten.

This storytelling work is remarkably, rewardingly healthy.
As we reveal ourselves in story, we become aware of the
continuing core of our lives under the fragmented surface of
our experience. As we become conscious of the multifaceted,
multi-chaptered *"I"* who is the storyteller, we can trace out the
paradoxical and even contradictory versions of ourselves that
we create for different occasions and different audiences—and
the threads that weave all these chapters, all these versions,
into one whole. Most important, as we become aware of
ourselves as storytellers, we realize that what we understand
and imagine about ourselves is a story. It is only one way of
representing our experiences, of composing and recomposing
our lives. Our stories are *not* the experiences themselves.

Psychologists tell us that this realization is deeply healing. In
order to make sense of what's happening in the chaotic and

often threatening external world, we create internal frames of reference, narrative structures: *stories*.

Sometimes our stories are affirmative and constructive, opening us to a generous and loving universe. Sometimes they are negative, limiting our choices, our actions, and our dreams, reflecting a universe that is more malignant than benign. Sometimes we actively define our stories: we portray ourselves as resourceful, hopeful persons capable of creating our own futures. Sometimes we passively allow our stories to define us: we see ourselves as persons with a confining past, persons without resources, without hope, victims of outside forces over which we have no control.

Understanding that our stories *are* stories—and hence open to radical retelling and revision—can help us begin to heal from the wounds that experience necessarily inflicts upon us as we grow and change.

This makes a good deal of sense, don't you think? When I can see the difference between the event and my story about it, between the experience and my interpretation of it, I can begin to glimpse the many creative means by which I author my own life. I become aware that my experiences, like stories, have a beginning, a middle, and an end. That my life, like all narrative, consists of plot, character, setting, theme—the fundamental constituents of story. When I have a feeling for the various plots and subplots of my life, the actions of the characters (including the main character, me!) begin to make psychological sense. When I understand how my actions lead from one result to another and another and another, I can see myself as the creator of my experience, of my life's plot. I can respect and admire my ability to compose an orderly existence out of the disorder and apparent randomness of events and influences that are a mystery to me when I am in their midst.

Our personal narratives, thoughtfully constructed, can have an enormously significant therapeutic potential. By reminding ourselves where we have been and what we have thought and what we have done, we can develop a clearer sense of what we might think and do in the future. The world seems rich with options and alternatives, and we have power and purpose. We can choose which potentials to realize—to make *real*—in our lives. We can *story* ourselves.

And more: As we remind ourselves of our stories, however painful, we soften the old scar tissue, solace aching miseries, and soothe bitter hurts. In telling the truth about our lives, we can cleanse the infection and close the open, painful wounds that have distorted us—that have kept us from realizing all that is possible for ourselves. And in sharing the truths, in opening our secrets together, our common wounds—women's wounds— may be healed.

The healing that can grow out of the simple act of telling our stories is often quite remarkable. Even more remarkably, this healing is not just our own healing: when it is shared, it is the healing of all women. That's why, as we tell our stories to ourselves, it is also important to share them with others. This sharing brings a sense of kinship, of sisterhood. We understand that we are not alone in our efforts to become conscious, whole, healthy persons. The more we learn about ourselves and our own lives, the more we want to know about the lives of other women—both women of our own time and place and women of other times, other places.

Stories have such enormous potential. When I tell you the story of my life, I don't have to do anything special—just tell the truth of it as I lived it, with all its ragged edges and loose ends, all the hurtful and the healing bits. When you tell me your story, I don't have to do anything special, either: just listen and accept, reflect, and be amazed. Together, telling and listening, accepting and reflecting, we are changed. Together, we reclaim the dynamic energy, the psychic power that is our inheritance. We can use that energy to compose ourselves in new ways, in astonishing new forms. We can empower ourselves and others to revise the script we were handed when we were born—the cultural script that tells women how to walk and talk and think and believe.

As we are discovering in this era of #MeToo, telling our true stories is indeed transformative—not only individually so, but collectively and culturally. We learn about women's experiences, we share those experiences, we are changed—and as we are changed, we can change the world. I am thinking here of the recent book, *She Said* by Jodi Kantor and Megan Twohey, about what happens in the workplace and throughout our culture when women's stories are truly told. Women's stories have never been more powerful than they are today, and the power of story—story power—has never been clearer.

The truth is that we yearn for honest, meaningful exchanges, the deep, human connection that authentic storytelling provides. We no longer gather around a campfire every night, but we continue to respond to the voice of a teller who engages us directly. In the past, it was often the women in the home who told the folktales, sang the songs, and remembered the tales of long ago. The art of storytelling today is practiced on many platforms and is inclusive, diverse, and personal. And through the technologies that allow those of us with access to the internet to publish our stories (in blogs, on social media and podcasts, and in author-published books), our voices are amplified.

And so *Story Power*, a how-to book on the art of storytelling, draws from the oral tradition and extends the invitation to become a storyteller to everyone who has a story to tell. Bringing the ancient tradition up to date with personal narratives of all kinds, author Kate Farrell guides us in the craft of creating and telling unforgettable, true stories for any occasion. With examples, prompts, and exercises in each thematic section, we are encouraged to explore significant events from our lives and those of our family. Farrell's work is not prescriptive: More than twenty skillful contributors with a range of diverse voices share their secrets to creating, crafting, and telling memorable tales, along with their narratives. *Story Power* is a handbook for discovering our own stories and finding our voices as storytellers in an enduring, ageless craft with tremendous potential.

Susan Wittig Albert, *New York Times* bestselling author and founder of the Story Circle Network

Susan Wittig Albert is the award-winning and *New York Times* bestselling author of *Loving Eleanor* (2016), a book about the intimate friendship of Eleanor Roosevelt and Lorena Hickok, and *A Wilder Rose* (2014), about Rose Wilder Lane and the writing of the Little House books. Her award-winning fiction also includes mysteries in the China Bayles series, the Darling Dahlias, the Cottage Tales of Beatrix Potter, and a series of Victorian-Edwardian mysteries she has written with her husband, Bill Albert, under the pseudonym of *Robin Paige*. She has written two memoirs: *An Extraordinary Year of Ordinary Days* and *Together, Alone: A Memoir of Marriage and Place*, published by the University of Texas Press. She is founder of the Story Circle Network, an international not-for-profit membership organization made up of thousands of women who want to document their lives and explore their personal stories through journaling, memoir, autobiography, personal essays, poetry, fiction, nonfiction, drama, and mixed media, based in Austin, Texas. Susan Wittig Albert is a member of the Texas Institute of Letters.

Foreword excerpts from the introduction of *Writing from Life: For Women with Stories to Tell* used by permission of the author.

Introduction

Say it.   Say it.
The universe is made of stories,
not of atoms.

— **"The Speed of Darkness" by Muriel Rukeyser**

Storytelling has been around as long as humans have.
The ancients of every culture told stories to make meaning
of life, to remember their history, and to entertain. A lot has
changed since then, but stories haven't. Some of the oldest
stories ever told are still with us—because it's in our nature to
both tell and listen to them.

In today's noisy, techie, automated world, storytelling is not
only relevant, it's vital. Without stories, we cannot connect to
each other. We lose something important; our humanity gets
lost in technology. Storytelling fills a crucial need in society
by providing a direct, personal connection through its art and
engaging oral tradition. But as the poet Rukeyser imagines of
us: *Do we struggle to get the live-bird out of our throat?*

Our stories don't exist on a printed page but in the images
we've stored in our minds. These pictures are fluid,
holographic, the instant replay loops of our experiences
and dreams. They are powerful: stories define us and create
the narratives that construct our lives. Personal stories are
universal: they illuminate our common ground and connect us
in compelling ways when we share them. The art of storytelling
helps us communicate with others and discover ourselves; it
inspires and emboldens us. By telling the pivotal stories of our
lives, we invite transformation.

Though storytelling is a legendary art, this book is a
straightforward guide, revealing the underlying secrets to
creating, crafting, and telling stories. In the spirit of traditional
storytelling, there are diverse voices in this book, since there
is no one way to tell a story. With more than twenty published
authors, memoirists, and storytellers, *Story Power* provides a
range of tips and illustrates the variety and appeal of personal
story. Enjoy this storytelling guide and add your unique voice,
wisdom, and wit to the ancient world of story!

How to Use This Book

Read the entire the book all the way through, or pick and choose from those chapters that most interest you. Chapters One, Two, and Three contain popular themes, three in each chapter, and are developed in depth. These three chapters follow a similar format and use icons to indicate each skill, illustrated by story samples. Chapter Four has storytelling delivery as its focus and can be applied to all story types. Chapter Five explores the rich heritage of folklore and how it might influence your personal stories and style.

Creating

This icon signals story selection—the creative process—and it is found throughout the book. It might appear next to the model story for a related theme or with a contributing storyteller's tips. If you are most interested in that part of the art, peruse the book for this icon.

Crafting

Crafting a story from raw experience is a careful process. This icon will guide you through the various ways that all the storytellers in these pages have honed their personal stories, along with an interpretive commentary. This section also includes a further deepening of story subtext in the discussions with the heading **Layers of Meaning**.

Telling

Preparing to tell a story is as important as its delivery. Preparation is discussed in the first three chapters, while the **Seven Steps** to skillful delivery are fully delineated in Chapter Five with graphic prompts.

Exercises & Prompts

All chapters contain prompts and exercises. Each chapter develops another aspect of the art of storytelling through its various themes. By participating in many of these story starters and exercises, you will find the tale types and stories that most fit your style and purpose. In doing so, you will find not only your authentic storytelling voice, but your essential truths.

Chapter One

Spinning Straw into Gold

And when the girl was brought to him, the king took her into a room which was quite full of straw, gave her a spinning wheel and a reel, and said, "Now set to work, and if by morning you have not spun this straw into gold, you must die." So there sat the poor miller's daughter, and for the life of her, she could not tell what to do—she had no idea how straw could be spun into gold.

—"Rumpelstiltskin" by the Brothers Grimm

Introduction

How do we take our raw experiences, half-remembered and fragmented as they are, and spin that seedy straw into the golden threads of a memorable story well told?

Whether you want to enliven a dinner conversation, engage an audience, roast a retiring colleague, or toast your best friend, a sparkling story will make you unforgettable while elevating the moment. The gold coinage of story adds value to everyday exchanges, either social or professional. The raw stuff of our life experiences can become entertaining, inspiring, or even motivating when shaped into a well-crafted tale and told with effective techniques.

It's true that we are surrounded each day by piles of straw: the mass substance of experience, the constant flow of incidents, the nonstop sensory impressions, and the emotional impact of it all. Our castle room is full up to the rafters.

How does each one of us as the magical alchemist—the storyteller—spin that material into gold? What experiences are not only vivid, memorable, laden with emotional charge, and personally significant but also have universal value? The golden thread is one that has a through line that connects the listener and the reader in a deeper way—a way that has value for both. These "golden" stories of lasting significance are not only encouraging but illuminating. That doesn't mean they are serious or solemn. Some of the best stories are told by stand-up comics.

Capture that thread! Spin your experiences for the telling. Share a signature story at a job interview or a childhood story on a date: personal stories are a way to immediately connect. And when they are crafted and well told, you'll engage your listeners so that they will remember you because they have identified with you.

In this digital age, most of us are hungry for meaningful, personal connection, now overtaken by instant texts and social media posts. We often reduce our communication to random headline links and memes. It's no wonder so many of us feel disconnected.

One of the problems of social media platforms is that they tend to depict "living your best life": travel, adventure, fine dining in the best clothes, or smiling families and friends at celebrations. There is a subtle competition that can leave those in a network of followers feeling less accomplished or appreciated—based only on snippets of photos and posts.

But you don't have to live an "exciting" life with exotic adventures or gourmet meals to be an engaging teller. That's not even relevant. What is key is the meaning you bring to what's happened—the gold you've spun from it. That way, the listeners see a glimmer of distillation—how you've extracted truth from your experience, one they understand and that resonates with them.

We are all a story, a life story. We may see people's stories more clearly after they've lived them to the end, when we know how everything turned out. But stories are just as exciting in the middle, when we don't know what's going to happen—when we are living each day. It would be good to share our stories with one another along the way, if only for the sheer entertainment of it; we might amuse each other with our predicaments. But sometimes it's hard to know how to begin.

So we mostly keep to ourselves and talk about the news, the weather, loose ends.

Some people seem to tell stories about themselves better than others. They're animated, amusing, entertaining, and so believable. When you listen to them, you're drawn right into the experience. What enables one person to tell stories and events better than another, personality aside, is the use of a few techniques that require some initial concentration. After you learn the basic dynamic that builds credibility, it becomes second nature. That is the art of storytelling.

This chapter will give you the techniques of effective storytelling for any setting: staff luncheon, public presentation, holiday gathering, or a long car trip. Use storytelling as a constant companion, one that is intriguing, interesting, and inviting. If you are practicing the art of storytelling, people seldom tire of listening. They'll stop what they're doing and fix a fascinated gaze on you until, of course, the story's over. Sharing yourself in stories might become a habit you won't regret.

Shaping and framing are the keys to telling your personal experiences as stories. Developing your own style is important, too, so you know how to tailor story content and structure to your delivery. If you have a slow and quiet style, you might work best with a few, well-chosen details, leaving the rest to the listeners' imagination. If you are a quick talker, you might embellish your tale with more imagery.

The truth is that each of us is already a storyteller. We've all had many memorable experiences—ones that we tell ourselves repeatedly in an inner monologue. Most of us have felt no one would listen because we've felt that what we have lived, or what we know, is neither interesting nor important. But just the opposite is true. What we can share with each other—a living experience through storytelling—is the most fascinating way we can communicate.

Storytelling can become the golden thread that weaves through our lives and binds us together.

Think of yourself for a moment as a *bon vivant*, a *raconteur*, a connoisseur savoring your own life. When you consider it, no one is going to fully enjoy and understand your life except you. And no one will know why they should unless you tell them. No one is likely to ask you for a childhood tale, or to reveal your most embarrassing moment, or explain why to this day, you feel queasy in an elevator. You'll find, however, that if you're discreet, telling your stories can make you a captivating, authentic personality.

It's vital to tune into your listeners in selecting a story to tell to a person or group at a particular time through the give-and-take of dialogue. Having a repertoire of your most memorable moments, told as stories, is an excellent way to participate in social conversation. Each time you learn to select, frame, and tell a true story, you become better able to do so almost instantaneously. You'll know the basic elements to create interest in a story that extends or enhances the topic at hand.

I remember that all through my young adult life, I felt humiliated by my childhood. I didn't want anyone to know where or how I was brought up—it seemed impoverished, shameful, even backward. So, I literally had nothing to say. Later, as I met successful people, I found if I scratched the surface of their lives, I often discovered an early life of poverty and struggle. The hard fact came home to me: most people are not born with the proverbial silver spoon in their mouths. Over the years, my shame has turned into a recognition and acceptance of everything that shaped and influenced me. All these experiences are simply part of who I am and the story I make of it.

Whatever has happened in your life, you've survived. So in a certain way, every story in your life has had a happy ending—you're here to tell about it and to enlighten your listeners. Your most miserable moments are worth telling because you've lived through them. It can be like "singing the blues": by the time you're singing them, you're on the way up. Storytelling is not only about the good times; it's about telling all the times worth remembering in your life.

Once you've gathered your personal story materials, what will you do with them? First, you can realize that you are interesting. Your life is full of color, feelings, drama, nuances, beauty, fear, dread, joy, elation, misery, and pain, as well as special objects, favorite hats, and worn-out teddy bears. And you might have thought you were boring or didn't have any stories to tell!

Next, you might want to blend your stories into everyday conversation, whether at a special occasion or in a public speech. As you practice the art of storytelling, use it often to prove a point or share a common experience. You'll become both convincing and entertaining—you might even earn a reputation for being wise.

Childhood & Coming of Age

The years from early childhood, the first flickers of memory, are precious. Yet they can often be difficult to capture. What if you've lost track of your story line? Where did it all start? Where is it going now? To get a sense of yourself and your own life story and to weave in those loose threads, take some time to reflect. Find an island of time where you can be alone with your thoughts. Turn off distractions—radio, TV, smart phone, and laptop. Just listen to yourself. Let your mind ramble comfortably for a while, then try to remember as far back as you can.

Recall your first memory, not what your parents or relatives have told you, but what you recollect. Fix that memory. Try to visualize it and sense as much as you can about it. Concentrate on the details of people, setting, dress, smells, and temperature. Summon tactile sensations: Were your socks itchy, your hands sweaty? Recall your emotions: What feelings did you have? What did you say? Remember as much as you can, then relax, let go. Let the images fade and vanish. This is hard work, but an important first step.

Replay your sense impressions of your first memories again. As you do, think of the beginning. How would you start if you were going to tell it as a story? You probably would want to introduce it with a few details of place, time, your age, the others involved, and their relationships. This gives your story a context, a setting, and its characters. Continue to the action. What was so compelling about it that made it worth remembering? Describe the experience in detail. How did it end? Now comes the most interesting part: the conclusion. What does the story say about you, what did you learn from it, or what did you learn about yourself in telling the story? There can be many conclusions: draw one.

As you build a repertoire of true-life story material, make it a practice to set aside time to quietly reflect on the memorable moments of your life—from the earliest impression to the present time. The more accurately you remember information, the more powerful your storytelling will be. There's nothing like an authentic sensory detail: The listener can feel its truth all the way to the bone.

Creating

The process of remembering and recalling is an inner journey into our young past: How do we retrieve the details, the dialogue, the feelings, and the meaning we made of it all?

A swirl of images and impressions can overwhelm us as we access childhood memories, a kaleidoscope of changing places, people, and moments. How do we fix on just one? Which one is a story, and which is simply a fleeting impression? Setting, where and when the event took place, is an essential part of storytelling and is often where we can start. A location or setting can sometimes be the dominant element in stories from our youth.

Listeners are curious about our origins and our roots—not to stereotype us, but to gain an understanding of our background, of the forces that influenced us. This is particularly true of stories from our childhood and youth. The early imprint of a place, with its culture, language, and weather, is formative and draws listeners in to learn more about us and connect.

For a childhood setting to stand on its own and tell a story, it needs to be substantial enough to answer these questions:

- What happened there?
- Was there a conflict, or was there rising tension?
- Did the main action occur over time with a clear progression?
- Were there other characters?
- Was there dialogue?
- Finally, was there a resolution?

If you can't answer these questions after lingering on this memory, then it's not a story, but just a remembered moment—a brief vignette.

For example, as I searched my mind for a childhood story, I focused on a time my family lived on the Mississippi Gulf Coast, where the most remarkable events happened in the little town of Pass Christian. Scanning through my first recollections, several came to the fore:

There was the time my older brother and I went crabbing on the public pier and came home with a bucket full of crabs. Mother filled the bucket with water and placed it on the stove's front burner on a high flame. When the water came to a boil, we watched as the crabs grew still.

This is a poignant memory, a mixture of joy at our crabbing success tainted with our squeamish reactions watching over the boiling bucket that killed the crabs. But there's not enough rise and fall of action for a compelling story. It's one of those throwaway incidents that typically start with, "I remember when..." These are wonderful as conversational tidbits, but not for storytelling.

Compare it to this memory; after careful reflection on its setting, it had enough elements to tell a story and even to set up a frame story:

The Secret Garden

Come with me, imagine with me, as we enter this incredible garden together. It must've been on a Saturday when us kids from the hardscrabble neighborhood along the back road decided to sneak into Middlegate Gardens again—a forbidden estate. The big house faced the Gulf of Mexico and its balmy breezes, a summer house for the rich folks from New Orleans.

That day, we slithered through the towering grove of bamboo that bordered one side of the garden until we came to the honeysuckle vine. There, according to ritual, we stopped, picked a flower, pinched it, pulled out the stem, and sucked its sweet nectar.

Making sure all was clear, we entered a place beyond our dreams: a huge, Japanese tea garden with stone lanterns, statues of strange creatures, a pagoda, a tea house, a guest house, ponds filled with slow-moving carp, tiny streams with curved, wooden bridges. Watching above it all was an enormous, seated Buddha up stone stairs, protected by two snarling temple guards, frozen in bronze. To us, it was our amazing playground.

The boys spread out for a silent game of hide-and-seek, but I, the only girl, crept closer to the big house, to find an empty swimming pool with a curvy shape. I could see glass doors in the house that opened to the garden and windows on the second floor, dark and quiet. I climbed down the rungs of the ladder into the shallow part. The pool was so large, a dry, cement floor, sloping down to its deep end, that I began to dance: spinning, twirling, and cutting a few fancy steps. But I kept glancing up to those dark windows, imagining someone there, watching me—a wicked child.

About then, the caretaker saw the boys running around and roared, "You damn kids! You get outta here!" A big, burly man, he chased after the boys who scampered away through the bamboo.

But he couldn't see me in the pool. I crouched in the shallow corner by the ladder and counted to a hundred. When all was quiet, I peeked over the edge. My heart pounding, I climbed out and ran. No one saw me dash across the wide expanse of lawn and through the scratchy bamboo.

Now, these many years later, the garden is gone, destroyed by hurricanes Camille and Katrina. Even the Buddha toppled from his high throne, decapitated and broken. Katrina, with her thirty-foot storm surge, obliterated the big house— swept it away along with the Japanese statues.

When I visited a few years ago, I saw the concrete foundations laid bare and the bamboo run wild. But now you know the secret that's whispering in the dry leaves: there was once a Japanese tea garden in all its exotic glory along the Mississippi Gulf Coast. In my memories, I tiptoe there still.

Crafting

To shape this story, I first spent hours refining my memories of that day, one of many times that we neighborhood children crept into the garden. With my eyes closed, I retraced our steps, squinting into my interior vision to recall that personal experience in as much detail as possible, so that the story rang true. I must admit my most vivid memories were the honeysuckle vine ritual and the fear of watchful eyes in the big house windows while dancing in that big, empty swimming pool—the impressions of a child.

Because the Middlegate Japanese Gardens were culturally unique and monumental in scope, I knew they must have a history. I wanted to make sure my memory was correct, that my girlhood impressions of its scale were accurate. A quick internet search found numerous descriptions of the gardens: a research paper, a recent book, and an online photo gallery in the Smithsonian Institute's Archival Repository of American Gardens.

The Buddha was, indeed, considered one of the largest in the world and sat on a twenty-foot high lotus pedestal. The swimming pool was designed to look like a natural lagoon, the miniature statuary depicted ancient idols or household elves, and the border groves were of a giant bamboo. I learned that the cottages along the back road where we lived, St. Louis Street, were once servants' quarters to the mansions that faced the Gulf. None of this exact research entered my story.

Nevertheless, I could be certain that I didn't dream this surreal place—it truly was as grand and amazing as I remembered. I could now claim it as a vivid, authentic memory. The Middlegate Gardens had a lifelong impact on me, and I grieved to learn of its tragic destruction.

Overall, research provides confidence to the teller as well as validation in verifying a childhood memory. But it does not replace direct, personal experience in shaping the story.

Layers of Meaning

As you select and craft a story worthy of telling, you'll discover there are elements and layers within it that might not be apparent at first. In choosing this particular story and giving it the title, "The Secret Garden," I found that, for me, there were many meanings to the word *secret*:

- The garden was forbidden and entered in secret

- The garden no longer exists except in secret memories and archives

- It was part of my secret, "shameful" past: a childhood in the Deep South

- Its total destruction in recent hurricanes is a secret in plain sight, that of climate change

And so, there are a variety of conclusions to be drawn from this story: loss, the impermanence of wealth and ostentation; the freedom and benefits of an unsupervised childhood; and climate change and the vulnerability of communities along the entire Gulf of Mexico. If I were an avid gardener, I would find other meanings in this tale. If I were a historian, I would find cultural significance in the remnants of French colonialism that radiated from New Orleans to coastal areas along the Gulf.

Telling

The conclusions you draw from a personal narrative determine how you'll tell the story, whether in social conversation, as an important story that demonstrates or introduces a point in a public presentation, or one that is appropriate for a family gathering.

Wherever or however you're going to tell the story, prepare to tell it by cutting its elements to the bone. Only by reducing any written draft version to a simple sequence of keywords or images will you be able to tell it without memorizing it. That is the art of the oral tradition.

Outline the story, stripping details down to keywords indicating its narrative arc.

For example, "The Secret Garden" has this outline:

1. Setting: Japanese tea garden at a summer mansion near New Orleans, along the Mississippi Gulf Coast

2. Characters: brother, age nine, neighborhood boys, ages six to ten, me, age seven

3. First scene, conflict: enter garden, bamboo grove, honeysuckle vine

4. Second scene, rising tension: boys hide-and-seek; I dance in empty pool, dark windows

5. Third scene, rising tension: chased out; boys run away

6. Fourth scene, climax: I hide in pool, wait

7. Resolution: I run away

8. Conclusion: Garden is still a secret

Keep the outline of a story in a story journal, on index cards, or by using a storyboard.

For more tools and techniques for telling and delivery, see Chapter Four for a story map, mind map, and storyboard, as well as the essential steps to telling.

The "Seven Steps to Storytelling" were original to the Word Weaving Storytelling Project and featured throughout its highly successful trainings for educators. They demystify the art of storytelling and break it down into easy-to-learn steps.

Exercises & Prompts: Childhood & Coming of Age

Storyline: Timeline

1. Choose a year in your early life, any year. With a year in mind, gather whatever memory aids you might have: photo albums, a childhood toy, an heirloom from that time.

2. Close your eyes and recall images of that year. Let them flicker off and on at random, then look for important events of that year. Choose one that had a problem, a conflict or tension, a drama.

3. Spend some time focusing on that event. See it, feel it, sense it, using all your senses. Feel your emotions. Think your thoughts.

4. Frame the impressions into a narrative arc: Visualize the first scene and see the action to the end.

5. Jot down the story notes in a journal. Use your own code or shorthand. Use sketches or other visual cues that will continue to unlock your memory of this story.

6. Tell the story to a close friend or relative. As you do, conjure up the images, details, feelings, and sensations that were part of the original event.

7. Tell it, don't talk it. For telling, the story must be well-lit with a freshness and immediacy, as if it were happening in the present.

Follow the Emotional Charge

1. If an incident still has an emotional charge from your youth, it's bound to include conflict or tension.

2. Remember a time when you were young, and you were scared.

3. Remember a time when you were young, and you were sad.

4. Remember a time when you were young, and you were happy.

5. Remember a time when you were young, and you were surprised.

6. Remember a time when you were young that was funny.

7. Remember another time when you were happy, and another time when you were sad, surprised, and/ or scared.

8. Now remember an event from one of those times that you would like to tell as a story.

9. When you have focused on that event, live through it again, and then open your eyes.

You may want to replay the story incident more than once. As you do, recollect sensory impressions, feel the emotions, and rehearse the dialogue.

Storytellers Share Secrets: Childhood & Coming of Age

The art of storytelling is ageless, timeless, and spans every culture. Personal narratives, especially of childhood and coming of age, can bridge many differences in their universal appeal. We can learn about the commonalities, challenges, and uniqueness of each one of us through our early stories. Set in their own time and place, we are able to live vicariously and walk in one another's shoes.

In addition, each storyteller has her own techniques in selecting and creating a personal story: There is no one prescribed way. In these three examples, we learn how other writers and tellers, memoirists and essayists, create a story, from an idea to a well-crafted tale. As you read these three approaches and story summaries, consider your own process of story discovery within the theme, "Coming of Age."

Creating

Sara Etgen-Baker has written over one hundred memoir and personal narrative essays, many of which have won awards and been published in e-zines, blogs, anthologies, and magazines, including WomensMemoirs.com, The Preserve, *Chicken Soup for the Soul, Guideposts, Table for Two, Inside and Out: Women's Truths, Women's Stories,* and *Times They Were A-Changing: Women Remember the '60s & '70s.*

Sifting Through the Sands of Time

Sara Etgen-Baker

It's funny how memories and moments flow away into the recesses of my mind, like grains of sand in an hourglass. Frequently, I feel like an archeologist digging and sifting through the sands of time, feverishly searching for a story to tell. Like any good archeologist, I've learned to be patient, for the challenge comes not in the sifting but in discovering *what* the story is. I inevitably select an event or story that evokes emotion and has either a memorable character, a pivotal moment, a message, or a grain of some universal truth. In the end, I want my story to transcend time and create an *aha* moment that makes the story meaningful to the reader.

When crafting the story, I look first to the setting and describe what happened, including details that evoke emotion. I introduce the conflicted protagonist who's on a journey, even if it's a minor one. I focus on a few key characteristics of my characters, allowing the reader to know each one in depth. I develop the plot with pivotal moments, creating a sequence that has rising tension, a narrative arc, and resolution. I employ dialogue, striving to show, not tell, placing the reader deep inside the story.

It's obvious from Sara's process of creating a story that she is experienced in doing so, and that she endeavors to affect some change in the reader or listener. Though she shares some standard tips, including beginning with the setting and adding characters, emotions, and dialogue, she also structures her story around the idea of a journey to develop the narrative arc. That Sara is interested in a journey, a message, and initiating a profound insight makes her narratives similar to a quest. We might anticipate that the main character will end up in a different place than where she began, and perhaps so will we.

Crafting

Ticket to Ride

Sara Etgen-Baker

I spent childhood summers with my unconventional Aunt Betty, who frequently pushed me into doing things that were uncomfortable. Such was the case one summer evening when she took my brother and me to the fairgrounds outside Cape Girardeau, Missouri.

"You gotta have a ticket to ride!" barked the carney. "Only two per chair. One of youz has to ride by yerself."

"She's the oldest; she'll ride by herself."

I sat down in my seat trembling, snapping the safety bar into place. The Ferris wheel bolted into action, slowly gaining momentum. The earth below me became smaller; the Ferris wheel stopped with me at the top. I gasped and closed my eyes. The wheel jolted forward, its rhythmic *rat-tat-tat-tuh* freeing my thoughts and lifting my spirit into the air. When we stopped, I opened my eyes and released the safety bar, stumbling and falling backward.

The following morning, I accompanied Aunt Betty to work, where she sat me in front of a manual typewriter and placed my hands on the home keys, demonstrating the reaches. "Here's my typing book. Follow the instructions." For days, I sat perched at the keyboard, practicing until boredom set in.

She handed me a box of picture postcards, suggesting, "Why not use these to create some stories?"

Over the summer, I typed several stories, carrying them home in a shoebox aptly labeled "Shoebox Stories."

I'd since forgotten about my Shoebox Stories until one day I uncovered a shoebox in my parents' attic and opened it—recognizing the faded words and images I'd created long ago. I realized that Aunt Betty gave me more than a ticket to ride a Ferris wheel: She gave me a ticket to ride above convention, past my fears, and into a life filled with anticipation and a level of inspiration that comes from having one's spirit set free.

Even in this condensed story summary, we sense a journey and an intense, personal change. The pivotal moments are not explained but are shown to us through sensory images and dialogue. The picture postcards from places unknown become more than their originally intended purpose. They are a ticket to the imagination of a young girl from her eccentric aunt, giving Sara permission to live outside the lines. Notice that the story details are commonplace: Ferris wheel, shoebox, typewriter, postcards, summer vacation. How such a combination of mundane items could become magical, even transformative, is in the meaning the teller brought to them.

We have the feeling that Sara would like us to open our own imaginary box of stories, ones written on "postcards" that depict memorable moments of our lives and jot them down. Doing so, we may understand our own journey: where we've been and where we're going. Sharing our stories with others is not only encouraging to our listeners but provides a new dimension to our lives. The published story was so popular that Sara was invited to read "Ticket to Ride" at the Starving Artist's Café in Little Rock, Arkansas.

Creating

Sheryl J. Bize-Boutte is an Oakland writer whose works artfully succeed in getting across deeper meanings about life and the politics of race without breaking out of her narrative. Her first book, *A Dollar Five: Stories From A Baby Boomer's Ongoing Journey* has been described as "rich in vivid imagery" and "incredible." Her latest book, *Running for the 2:10*, a follow-up to *A Dollar Five*, delves deeper into her coming of age in Oakland and the embedded issues of race and color.

Sheryl J. Bize-Boutte

Almost all of my autobiographical writings utilize the short story form. My initial considerations for writing stories about my coming of age include:

- What pivotal occurrence found within a memory helped to shape me and continues to form me as my unique self

- How much of the setting, people, and surroundings are historically important, relevant events that I remember or can research

- How rich I can make it with the right words within the confines of a short story

- How compelled I am to share the story with others

I follow the tenets above and let it flow. As I am writing, one of the most important things I consider is that these are *my* memories, in my voice, and told when I am ready to tell them. This is important for coming-of-age stories. If a writer is telling her truth, that is all there is. And after all of that, I put on my professional writer's hat and edit for clarity and fullness of meaning. And when I finish and read it over for the last time, if I cry, frown, smile, or laugh out loud at the memory, I know I have done my job.

Sheryl's process for story selection illustrates the elements of good storytelling in personal narrative: pivotal event, authenticity, unique voice, emotional tone. But her choice includes another important criterion, that of historical and social context. As an African American, she chooses to use as a story component the societal issues that defined her during her coming of age, rather than ignoring them. This not only brings her truth to each story but allows us to identify with her experiences and see the racial divide from her side. That she does so with clarity and honesty is a tribute to Sheryl as a gifted storyteller. Sharing personal stories can create a platform for cultural and racial understanding and is a power in itself.

Crafting

A Dollar Five

Sheryl J. Bize-Boutte

As a twelve-year-old African American girl coming of age in Oakland, California, in the 1960s, I was aware of both the subtleties and harshness of discrimination—always evident. During this timeframe, Oakland was still about three years from the completion of white flight, while the more visible manifestations of the Civil Rights Movement in our hometown were just a whisper away.

Although this was a tense and fluid time, Oakland was still richly diverse, and I had schoolmates of almost every ethnic background and color. My best friend at that time was white. She and I mostly ignored the changes going on around us and had a bond that we felt could not be broken by the dumb grown-ups on the evening news who could not seem to get along. We thought that until a fateful day on our first trip to the movies, when she sat in the balcony with the white kids and I sat in the floor seats with the black kids. It became clear to us once we arrived at the neighborhood theater that this segregation was automatic, and we had no choice. But it was not the right thing to do for two friends. We knew we could not sit with each other, and so we stayed in our places for the duration of the film. We had not considered how it would make us feel. It was the decision she made that day after the movie was over that changed my life and hers forever. The memory of her and her stance would become the basis of my short story, "A Dollar Five," as well the title of my first book.

Sheryl leaves us hanging by a thread at the end of this dramatic story summary. But if we think about it for a minute, we know what happened, what stance her friend took—though perhaps not in so many words. That Sheryl doesn't spell it out gives her friend's unnamed courage more impact. We have to step inside the story and enter that moment, fill it with our own sense of compassion or justice. Nevertheless, I had to purchase the e-book edition of *A Dollar Five*. The published ending was equally as subtle. It brought home to me that small actions can be heroic and create change, that bravely reaching out to a friend can occur in a simple, everyday moment and make all the difference. I also notice in the synopsis above that Sheryl effectively uses two voices: as a girl and as an adult, with her adult voice appearing at the introduction and at the end, as the narrator to the story. It is no surprise that as an expressive and exciting teller, Sheryl has been said to "bring down the house" with live presentations of her short stories and poems.

Motifs in Storytelling

What was stunning to me in these two personal stories is that both used a similar motif, that of a **ticket.** As a literary device, a motif is a recurring narrative element with symbolic significance, one that connects to the "big idea" in the work. In both stories, the ticket is a literal one, purchased to enter both the Ferris wheel and the movie theater. Yet both storytellers repeat the same pattern or motif as a symbol: a ticket opens the door (or gate) to a wider, bigger world. Neither Sara Etgen-Baker nor Sheryl J. Bize-Boutte know each other, and they live thousands of miles apart. This was a random phenomenon, or was it?

There are universal patterns in the oral tradition, something that no one can truly explain. In Chapter Five, we'll take another look at motifs and other elements within the worldwide heritage of folklore. You might be surprised to find story motifs or even archetypes that occur in your own work.

In these two personal stories, we could be inspired to use the **ticket motif** for a coming-of-age story as a prompt for one of our own: *When did a ticket to travel or to an event change your young life?*

Creating

Jing Li is originally from China. Her soon to be published memoir, *Red Sandals*, is a coming-of-age, survival story in a country that devalues female infants. Her mother tried to abort her, then abandoned her; Jing was raised by her paternal, peasant grandmother, who was inclined toward infanticide of female babies and had no use for girls. Later, when Jing herself gave birth to a girl, her father-in-law pressured her to have her infant daughter lethally injected. Her personal narratives have won awards: the Grand Prize in the San Francisco Writing Contest sponsored by the San Francisco Writers Conference; First Place, CWC, Redwood Branch Memoir Contest; the True Grit Award of the Mt. Hermon Writers Conference; and Second Place in Nonfiction in the CWC Jack London Writers Contest. Jing's personal stories have been published in numerous anthologies.

Jing Li

After writing the first few of my childhood stories, I soon became restless. Which stories should I select from the myriad of memories of my youth to shape my memoir? "Well," advised one memoir teacher to me, "Just keep writing." It was 1999. There was very little how-to-write-a-memoir guidance available then.

So, I wrote on, blindly, one story at a time, with no chronological order or purpose, just whatever memory burst out to me, one I had a burning desire to tell next. After eight years of such random writing, while working full time, I gradually saw the pattern or the theme for my memoir: survival, resilience, and triumph. This theme was acknowledged in my first American writers' award in 2007: Second Place in the California Writers Club's Jack London Writers Contest.

When I write, I keep my audience in mind. Their nodding of understanding and sympathy and their smiles of encouragement were healing for my traumatized childhood. The positive feedback and insightful questions from well-intentioned fellow writers were memory-triggering and mind-nurturing. Almost all my memoir chapters stemmed from the dozens of writers' critique groups, open mics, and writers' conferences I attended during my twenty-year writing endeavor.

Jing Li began writing personal narratives when memoir was a new genre, simply motivated by an impulse to make sense of her life in China through stories. It is quite clear that the writing community provided her with live audiences for listening, critiques, and help with her revisions. Jing's background as an educator gave her the confidence to share her personal stories on stage, at open mics, or in critique groups. That she was willing to seek them out, to pursue live critique, shows her determination to not only create authentic, well-crafted stories, but to do so with immediate feedback. Though she found support and validation among her writing colleagues, she braved their criticism as well.

Crafting

Jing Li

I selected "My Childhood Laughter with Lao Ye Ye" because it's a peek at a rare, shining jewel in my grim, growing up years as a peasant girl born unwanted in a remote mountain village in China—where happiness was as rare as food, water, or clothes. It turned out to be the audiences' all-time favorite. I've told it to many hundreds of people at numerous open mics from California to Wisconsin to Iowa.

It was a real challenge to craft a well-structured story from my "shitty first draft," as someone once called it. Searching my memory long and hard, I tried as faithfully as possible to record the dialogue and describe the scenes and its historical background. Then I would step back and let it sit for days, weeks, even months, before coming back to edit, reedit, and revise many times over, chiseling a diamond from the rough. Brevity is the essence. Such has been my tortoise-in-the-race, memoir-writing journey.

My Childhood Laughter with Lao Ye Ye: Synopsis

My great-grandfather Lao Ye Ye lost his eyesight after toiling in the cornfields all his life. Confined indoors, he became my daytime refuge when I was barely one year old.

My happiest memory was giggling and laughing with Lao Ye Ye playing our favorite game, "Taking Lao Ye Ye to the Main Street." Giggling secretly, I'd tiptoe, leading my blind great-grandpa straight to the dead corner of the yard.

"This is not the Main Street!" Lao Ye Ye would act surprised, his walking cane poking at the river rock stone wall. I'd burst out laughing. "You tricked your Lao Ye Ye. Get over here, my darling little rascal." Lao Ye Ye opened his arms, waiting to reward me with his loving hugs.

My laughter was buried with my beloved Lao Ye Ye when I was five.

Though Jing Li compressed this favorite story into a short form, its impact is intense. As Jing mentioned, "brevity is the essence." Each detail is critical and creates setting, character, structure, and final resolution. We learn the context for her story in the brief introduction: that the setting is a remote mountain village in China; that she was unwanted and neglected from birth; that peasant life was harsh with constant poverty and toil. Yet the bond shown here between two abandoned members of the extended family is both endearing and transcendent. What is effective in Jing's storytelling style is that she steps out of the way of the story. By entering directly into the action with convincing dialogue, we are suddenly there. We identify with the games of pretend of the very young and the indulgence of the elderly. These compelling universals made this narrative an all-time favorite: a tale of treasured childhood moments in a bleak environment.

Adventure Stories

Call it the global village: the world is shrinking. We are more connected than ever before, with live news coverage and the means to travel to faraway locations. But is our understanding of people, cultures, and history increasing? As we journey along well-worn tourist paths or to far-flung destinations, we are eyewitnesses to the marvels of our planet. If we not only gather photos and mementos, but chronicle our adventures with well-told stories, we can bring a unique perspective to our experiences. Sharing tales of what we learned and saw on the ground can bridge the gap between cultures and entertain our listeners.

In the time-honored tradition of the itinerant storyteller, often called a bard, a teller would entertain a household or village with exotic stories of travels and oral history in exchange for food and lodging. Long before the printed press or social media, these tellers were a living network, and they existed worldwide: they were found among the Russian traditions of the "kaleki," the "ntsomi" tellers of Africa, the storytellers of the "yose" and "kodanshi" of Japan, the "Bankelsanger" of Germany, and the "dakkalwars" of India, not to mention Native American tale-tellers of such diverse tribes as the Clackamas Chinook, Navajo, Jicarilla Apache, and Winnebago. So you, too, can join the ranks of these legendary bards and charm your friends and audiences with epic tales of your journeys and feats.

But how do we create compelling stories from the hundreds of photos, videos, and impressions we've gathered from our latest trip or adventure? In a counterintuitive process, it is better to focus on the people, not the places. Use your laser eye to zoom in on a dramatic moment of tension with the people you met or with your travel mates. If you simply arrange a commentary around your itinerary with a slide show of photos, you will flatten the storyline. Describing when and where you went step-by-step will only bore your listeners: you will not have reflected on your experience in a way that deepens both your own experience and theirs.

Just as a setting can be the hook for childhood stories (illuminating your place of origin), so an adventure tale is worth telling because of its drama and intriguing characters. As you recall the people in your travels, think of their dialogue, the way they spoke, their personalities, and their style. Even if you don't use all these details, you'll be able to select some. Once you shift your focus to the people, not the places, you'll have the beginnings of a good tale.

The old-time bards told heroic tales of high drama, often in verse. **No one expects you to intone your tale in verse or song, but we do expect to be entertained and amazed— to vicariously live a moment on the edge.**

Crafting

As you search through your adventurous memories, let them play on your inner movie screen. Which people catch your eye? Which characters—not places—are the most compelling? Then consider what made them so memorable. They might have said something wise, or they may have been part of a crisis or an unforgettable moment.

Review your purpose: why do you travel or adventure? If you can honestly answer that question, you'll be able to find a purpose in your storytelling. The common reasons to adventure or travel are to broaden your horizon, change your perspective, gain new cultural understanding, deepen your life, or learn new skills. If some of these are your reasons, then your stories will offer those enriching qualities to those who hear them. Listeners want to know how you were changed—what encounters were significant enough to share.

For an adventure story to have the essential elements for telling, answer these questions:

- What was the most dramatic moment of your trip?
- People: Who was there? Describe.
- Who or what threatened your life or well-being?
- What was said? Recall dialogue.
- What was the narrative arc: conflict, rising action, tension, resolution?
- What did you learn, or what question(s) did you ask?

If your memory can't provide these elements, then it is only a vignette, not a full-blown tale. If you were telling it for your supper, you'd go away hungry, and so would your listeners.

For example, as I searched my recollections for a wild adventure story, I focused on a trip to the Galapagos Islands, off the coast of Ecuador. Famous for the studies Charles Darwin made there that led to his theories of evolution, they remain a remote and primal place. This scene came to mind:

One morning, the naturalist guide joined us over breakfast in the cabin of the seventy-two foot sloop, saying he had a surprise, but we had to promise to be absolutely quiet. The ten of us climbed down to the *panga*, the outboard, for a wet landing on an uninhabited island. He gestured for us to hide behind the sand dunes and wait. Slowly, the mists that typically formed during the night began to dissipate like a curtain rising on a play, revealing hundreds upon hundreds of bright pink flamingos feeding on the krill in an inland lagoon. With their heads upside down in the shallow water, they reminded me of the flamingos in *Alice in Wonderland* when Alice used their heads as mallets in a game of croquet.

No doubt, this is a charming memory, but is it transformative? It is definitely worthy of a slide show comment, as it shows a fascinating scene unfolding. But even with some interaction and a literary reference, it doesn't rise to the level of a tale. There is no conflict—no drama. This vignette is so pleasant as to be completely flat.

Compare it to this memory centered on the people who were in our tour: the characters and their issues and conflicts are the drama, while the islands are a backdrop. Ideally, the location could become an essential part of the action, even another character, due to its symbolic or historic meaning.

Christmas Cruise 1980

"Mutiny!" they cried as they approached me on the sloop's main deck. "We're going to mutiny!" I'd watched a group of four emerge from the cabin and pick their way across the swaying boat in the dark. No place to hide—I listened to their complaints while pulling up my halter top in the sea breeze.

"Why should we be stuck out here on Christmas Eve—abandoned by our naturalist guide?" Irene said.

"Yeah, all the guides anchored their boats so they could go ashore and party. That's just not right." her friend agreed.

We were among several tour boats anchored off the island of Santa Cruz in the Galapagos Archipelago, one of the most remote spots on earth, where Darwin developed his theories of evolution.

"So, what do you expect me to do?" As their appointed escort guide and the only one who spoke passable Spanish, I glanced around uneasily.

"Hear those drums? We're going dancing! There's a rooftop bar with live music over in Puerto Ayora. Check this out!" Dan urged me to look through his high-powered binoculars across the water.

"Okay, okay! I'll go find the *capitán.* I'll see if somebody can take us over in the *panga.* But it's probably going to cost us." I threw on a summer dress, and, minutes later, the five of us went roaring across the quiet waters of Academy Bay in the outboard—the *capitán* pocketing our money and depositing us on a wooden dock.

Seated on tree stumps around a small table on the uneven rooftop, we drank beer in the sultry night, toasting our mutinous success. Changing partners, we danced to the band and a lively drumbeat. Our beers gave way to rum and Coke. But when the club closed down just before midnight Mass, we wandered the deserted island paths while the church bells rang for Christmas.

Irene stumbled on the rocks. "Oh NOOO, he'll be singing in the cathedral now." Irene wept for her gay friend who sang with her in a symphony chorus: "He'll never love me as I love him." Her wails pierced the still night.

"Shush. It's time to meet *capitán* at the dock," I said. Subdued, we walked to the dock and waited, and waited. No one came—we were stranded again.

Now what? I knew they expected me to do something. They moved away as a solitary woman, an Ecuadorian, dressed in black with a long braid of black hair, walked to the end of the dock. I greeted her in my halting Spanish and told her we were stuck.

She was shy, kind, and whispered, *"Mi esposo viene— te llevará."*

I expressed my gratitude that her husband could give us a ride back to the boat and beckoned to my group. A thick mist was forming over the water, and I strained to hear the guttural sound of a motorboat. But it was a longboat that appeared silently through the mist, rowed by none other than the legendary Gus Angermeyer—one of the original settlers, a German who had fled the Nazis back in the 1930s. I suppose I gushed as we clambered aboard; I was effusive in my thanks when we reached the sloop.

"Ach! You talk too much." Gus smiled. I took that to mean *Don't mention it.*

On board, I went searching for the *capitán.* I found him in the pilothouse, weeping over his estranged *esposa* and *familia.* Overcome with emotion and drink, he was beyond scolding. Frustrated, I returned to the main deck alone, pondering the night's events and human evolution.

Is yearning part of evolution? Do we always want what we can't have? Is that why we wiggled out of the sea on rubbery legs: because we yearned for more, because we wanted to dance, sing, love?

Or maybe—we just talk too much.

Crafting

To develop this tale, I spent time with my eyes closed, seeing the action play out in my mind's eye. To my surprise, I recalled the people, their appearance, and the dialogue almost immediately, as if it had happened yesterday. Obviously, this was a Christmas Eve to remember. That it happened in a wild place, semi-inhabited, in the middle of nowhere, created a vulnerability that heightened the experience. That I was left onboard with demanding clients as the responsible adult added to my stress. These were imprints that lit up that evening in bright lights—the electric charge of emotion.

Though I could imagine the personal dramas, I'd lost track of exact place names and background facts. In particular, I knew only bits and pieces of the Angermeyers' flight from Nazi Germany. With a brief search, I discovered it was at the urging of their parents that these young men fled Germany. In 1935, the Angermeyers sold their home in order to purchase the yacht on which five brothers sailed away from Hamburg and Hitler. They first went to Holland, but, after a shipwreck off the coast of England, only four of the five made it to the sparsely inhabited islands. In 1937, Karl, Gus, Hans, and Fritz Angermeyer arrived on Santa Cruz Island, where they lived like Robinson Crusoe. After the death of Fritz, it was the surviving three brothers who envisioned a post-war tourist trade to the Galapagos.

It was important for me as the teller to know the backstory of these most famous settlers. It underscored their mystique:

how it was Gus who magically came to the rescue, a bigger-than-life man, rowing all of us with ease—why his few words had such an impact. Equally important were the details of the sloop and the unique place in history of those famed islands. But once I'd refreshed my memory with relevant information, I added only a few key details to the story so that the action and characters dominated.

Layers of Meaning

This adventure took place on islands where humans are the visitors and wildlife is friendly—a land before time. With harsh, lava landscapes under a fierce, equatorial sun, the islands themselves became a "character" in my story. They brought to mind the big picture of the origin of life on earth, who we are as a species, and where we're headed. It seemed to me that the flora and fauna of the Galapagos Islands, having been observed, make us observe, measuring our human progress.

Christmas Eve is of enduring importance in Western European culture. Aside from its religious significance, it is a holiday of great expectation. The characters in this story felt cheated—they expected that the Christmas Cruise should have given them holiday joy. The wellspring of emotions that Christmas evokes is universal: nostalgia, regrets, disappointments—the sense that we haven't been good enough, after all. The holiday has a strong presence in this tale, even though it occurred on the equator, where there is no change of seasons or in the length of days.

All of these layers and more are part of this story. The trick is to give meaning to the story as you tell it, not

in the text, but in the subtext. How you set the emotional tone is what is said between the words. When you reflect on a personal story and discover its layers of meaning, you'll be able to incorporate the dimension of tone and implied meaning in your telling.

The meaning you bring to an adventure story will influence its style and tone as well as how and where you'll tell it. The exact same tale could be told with humor, tension, or deep reflection. Like a chameleon, the story could change based on where you tell it: in dinner conversation, around a campfire, or in a more formal presentation. It can become longer or shorter, like a telescope.

Wherever or however you'll going to tell the story, prepare to tell it by cutting its elements to the bone. Only by reducing any written, draft version to a simple sequence of keywords or images, will you be able to tell it without memorizing it word-for-word. That is the flexibility of the oral tradition.

Telling

Outline the story, stripping details down to keywords indicating its narrative arc.

For example, Christmas Cruise 1980:

1. Setting: Galapagos Island of Santa Cruz, Christmas Eve, 1980

2. Characters: shipmates, crew, islanders, Gus Angermeyer

3. First scene: a group mutinied when our sloop was anchored in Academy Bay

4. Second scene: bribing the *capitán* to take us ashore in the *panga* (motorboat)

5. Third scene: partying at the rooftop club

6. Fourth scene: after hours, wandering and weeping, stranded

7. Fifth scene: Gus Angermeyer appeared out of the mist in his longboat

8. Sixth scene: *capitán* drunk and weeping in the pilothouse, unaware

9. Resolution: back on main deck, pondering, is yearning part of evolution?

Note the rising action for each scene, and a pattern in the main action and its resolution. Keep the outline in a story journal, on index cards, or by using a storyboard.

Refer to Chapter Four to find more tools for preparing to tell a story, along with techniques for delivery.

The "Seven Steps to Storytelling" were original to the Word Weaving Storytelling Project and featured throughout its highly successful, professional development trainings for educators. These demystify the art of storytelling into easy-to-learn steps.

Exercises & Prompts: Adventure Stories

Storyline: Character Benchmarks

1. Create a timeline for your adventure or trip, based on your travel itinerary

2. Pinpoint the times you met interesting people

3. Describe them with expressive details, including dialogue

4. Define their significance in your trip

5. Jot down the interaction and the drama

6. Create a list of these people throughout your trip or adventure

7. Jot down their names or roles in a story journal

Follow the Action

With your timeline close at hand, along with some of your photos, videos, or slides, recall:

1. A moment of tension, conflict, or fear

2. Remember another time of fear or tension

3. Recall another moment when you didn't know what would happen next

4. Think of a time when you were confused or lost

5. Remember a time when you were threatened or confronted

6. Think of a time when you were shocked

7. Recall a time when you became ill or had an accident

8. Think of a successful moment of accomplishment or skill

9. Focus on one event that has the elements of a complete story

When you have selected one event, replay it in your mind's eye more than once. As you do, focus on who was there, what they looked like, and what they said. Feel your emotions; identify the main conflict and its resolution. Draft a written story to give your tale shape and substance using keywords and dialogue. Use the organizing tools in Chapter Four to plot the narrative and to prepare for telling.

Storytellers Share Secrets: Adventure Stories

Travel writers know that the destination is not the story. Wherever they go, they need to think like a journalist and dig out the story; that could mean interviewing people on the ground to search one out. Since you are not a travel writer but a traveler, you will most likely meet people on a random basis. Nevertheless, you can reach out to people along the way and seek out their stories.

No one wants to hear every detail of your travel experiences, no matter how fascinating or challenging you might have found them. Use a bright spotlight to recall the dramatic moments.

You might even be alert to the appeal of a crisis while it's occurring and jot down a few notes or record the incident on your mobile device.

Every travel article uses a hook: an event or a theme. When you sort through your adventure memories, find the hook. It may not be evident until you reflect. If there is a theme, organize your stories to develop it. **Your listeners will never forget your travel stories because they will have internalized them, lived through their truths, and survived along with you.**

Creating

Lisa Alpine is an award-winning travel writer, a dancer, and a wild woman. Her online magazine features adventure travel and other tales of inspiration. Recent awards include: Solas Gold 2019 Best Travel Memoir for "Ole in Paris"; Bronze Best Humor 2019 for "The Twerking Nun of Korce"; Honorable Mention 2019 for "Where God, Anchovies, and Flamenco Reside"; and Best Women's Travel for "Sugar Granny and Her Dancing Shoes." Her story "Fish Trader Ray" received the Silver Solas Medal for Best Travel Story of the Year.

Wanderlust

Lisa Alpine

My adventure stories are woven from the threads of wanderlust that are the fabric of my life. I am a woman who wanders and wonders and writes. I have no room for souvenirs in my backpack, but I do have stories to share and a desire to tell them. Translating the world through story and dance has always been my launch pad and my anchor. Both art forms are my bliss.

I suggest finding your bliss and the focus of your passion. Gardening? Rock climbing? Salsa dancing? Weave your stories around a nugget, a nut, a kernel of an experience that is woven from your passion. This fire will hold your audience captive. Passion is contagious and ignites the soul.

Other guidelines I use in selecting a story are:

• Is it timely? Related to a world event or holiday?

• Who is my audience? Adventurous young women who want thrills? School children who love animals? A self-awareness or spiritually oriented group who need an insightful, uplifting, or perhaps mystical story?

• How much time is allotted for the presentation?

Lisa's award-winning success as a travel writer is a good indication that readers love to feel drama, passion, and fire in an adventure story. Not only is she aware of what her readers desire, but what she wants as a traveler. No doubt, she journeys with her eyes and heart wide open to the world. Though you might not be clear on your storytelling audience until your return, you will be able to adapt the raw material of your experience for a variety of listeners, from family members to a professional group.

Crafting

Fish Trader Ray

Lisa Alpine

The early morning sun was already blazing on the Amazonian frontier town as I walked the wooden sidewalk that went back toward Leticia. Electric Blue Morpho butterflies burst from the rain puddles while mangy mongrels skulked about, picking at piles of fish bones haloed in clouds of botflies. Indians in feathered headdresses and ear plugs, their skin painted in red *achiote*, hustled past on their way to the open-air market, carrying spider monkeys, black caimans, emerald-green macaws, and even a terrified hissing jaguar kitten, trussed on poles or trapped in basket cages swinging from the Indians' blowguns.

One shirtless *mestizo* in ragged soccer shorts had a twelve-foot anaconda draped around his shoulders. He caught sight of me and, before I could wave him off, he wrapped the snake around my neck, holding onto the back of its head so it couldn't bite, and asked for money for a photo. The reptile was uncomfortably weighty and smelled of snake urine, which has its own distinctly unpleasant pungent odor. As I looked at its skin, I noticed ticks bloating out from underneath its scales. Repulsed, I wiggled out of the snake's tightening grip.

Bursts of gunfire, coming from a ramshackle bar perched on stilts overhanging the river, punctuated the cacophony at the dock. This roughshod town assaulted all of my senses at once, invoking Hieronymus Bosch's paintings of hell. Salty sweat poured down my face, stinging my eyes. I managed to make my way to the deserted main plaza and sat, panting, on a bench under the pathetic shade of a scrawny palm tree. Scratching under my shirt, concerned one of the ticks had hopped off the snake for a warmer host, I wondered how to find Ray. He didn't have a phone or an address, and he had simply told me, "When you get to Leticia, just ask for Fish Trader Ray."

I motioned to a young boy kicking a ball across the otherwise-empty plaza. "*Dónde está* Fish Trader Ray?"

The boy looked puzzled and then asked, "*Pescadero Raymundo?*"

He motioned for me to stay where I was and ran off down a side street. Minutes later, Ray appeared on an exhaust-spewing motorcycle with his wife and several kids hanging off his wide girth like a bunch of ripe bananas.

This excerpt from Lisa's story "Fish Trader Ray," published in *Wild Life: Travel Adventures of a Worldly Woman,* **has many elements Lisa says people love: "outrageous characters, danger, humor (usually self-deprecating), animals, exotic locale, poetic ending**." Ray was a tropical fish trader Lisa met on her first day in Bogota, Colombia. They agreed to meet in Leticia, Colombia, to plan a trip down the Amazon River. Her descriptive style skips through a variety of sensory impressions, giving us the most startling ones. She deftly places us in a strange locale using a few critical details—just enough to bring us to the feathered Indians and the shirtless *mestizo* with the repulsive snake. Ask yourself, what was the most vivid detail in this passage: Was it the butterflies or the reptile? With the brief description of Fish Trader Ray, what do you anticipate on his Amazonian river tour?

Creating

Simona Carini was born in Perugia, Italy, and now lives in Northern California. Simona writes nonfiction and poetry, has been published in various venues in print and online, and has won awards for her memoirs and food writing. Her narrative, "The Blue Backpack," was published in the 2015 Redwood Writers' anthology *Journeys* and reprinted in the 2016 California Writers Club *Literary Review*.

Simona Carini

I start with a physical object that elicits vivid and emotional memories in me—an object that wants to tell its story. My first draft is the story as I know and/or remember it, with a focus on the object's protagonist. I write with no predefined plan to avoid editing while I am still writing.

In subsequent drafts, I add context to frame the story, sensory details to bring it closer to the readers' experience, and snippets of dialogue to give life to the characters involved. In parallel, I work on the story arc, the conflict or tension that drives the narrative forward and affects the characters. That is what keeps interest alive as the story unfolds.

I don't at first ask the question, "What's the story about?" But I must arrive at that answer before I begin editing, because what I keep and what I delete during that process depends on the answer.

Audiences should be able to relate to the story: this is the focus driving the final revisions. They may have had a similar experience, know someone who has, or in other ways they should feel a kinship with the teller throughout the story.

Simona's process offers us a unique way to begin a personal narrative: with an object. This focus could easily relate to a travel or adventure experience. A found object, or one purchased as a souvenir or memento, could become a story prompt: show and tell! For example, if you sought and brought a Murano glass pendant with a millefiori design, you might first write about the piece with its history and the techniques used to make it, then add the moment of discovery: the setting, the people, the atmosphere of the place. Was there a conflict, a tension about the object, before, during or after its purchase? Finally, what is the arc of the story—the revelation of the personal and/or symbolic meaning of the piece? That it cost far too much, but you overspent anyway? Or did the pendant cause friction with a travel mate? As you share your tale about an object from your adventure, you might include it—now infused with meaning.

Crafting

The Blue Backpack: Story Synopsis

Simona Carini

I was born and grew up in Italy, while Robert, my husband of twenty-two years, was an American. We have been asked many times to tell the story of how we met. He relishes narrating the details of the fateful encounter, which happened at a conference held in a hotel outside Amsterdam. He surprises the audience by saying that he knew I was "the one" when he saw my blue backpack perched on top of a collection of black roll-aboard bags belonging to the conference attendees.

When it is my turn to tell the story, I start with my blue backpack. It reflects who I am—it brought my husband and me together and was the leitmotif of my move from Italy to California.

My parents were taken by surprise by my decision, though my move to Northern California followed a pattern of not adhering to what was traditionally expected of me.

The blue backpack carried all my belongings. The experience of packing for a long, one-way journey is shared by all immigrants, regardless of the reasons behind their move. I had to decide what would come with me—a special dress, a stuffed animal, my fountain pen—and what would stay.

My preparations culminated in a long intercontinental flight and the arrival to a new home. My newfound life began, and I encountered obstacles: my excellent English sometimes was not good enough, and I had defied expectations, so talking with my friends in Italy was no longer easy. I dealt with such difficulties with Robert's help and his love for me.

My American dream of the heart came true, which is where the tension of the story comes to rest. And I still have the blue backpack: it travels with me and it continues to tell its story.

It's fascinating that so much personal meaning and romance could fit in an ordinary backpack. Yet it was distinctive, set apart from all the rest of the luggage: a bright blue defiance among the conventional, black wheeled suitcases. Even in this condensed version of the longer tale, we sense the tenderhearted encounter that became a bond between the two adventurers at the conference in Amsterdam. The wanderer motif is further amplified when Simona packs all her belongings in the backpack to travel from Italy to her new love's home in Northern California. Hers is the quest of the immigrant going against the expectations of friends and family to seek her dream. And the stories of the blue backpack continue. There is a folk tradition of the story sack used by the itinerant storyteller with charms inside that represented stories. So, you, the modern traveler, can collect mementos along the way—and use each one to tell a story of your experiences; it's better than a slide show.

Creating

Mary Mackey is the author of fourteen novels, including The *Village of Bones* and *The Year the Horses Came*, which describe how the peaceful Goddess-worshiping people of prehistoric Europe fought off patriarchal nomad invaders. Mary's novels have made *The New York Times* and *San Francisco Chronicle* bestseller lists, have been translated into twelve foreign languages, and have sold over a million and a half copies. Mary is also the author of eight collections of poetry, including *The Jaguars That Prowl Our Dreams*, winner of the 2019 Erich Hoffer Award for the Best Book Published by a Small Press and a 2018 Women's Spirituality Book Award.

Mary Mackey

A sense of audience is your most important asset:
Whether I am writing a personal story, a poem, or a novel,

I am always intensely aware of my audience. I select stories that are exciting, stories my readers will find interesting, informative, and entertaining. I resist the urge to write diary-like entries of interest only to me.

Never bore your audience: I work hard to make reading my stories easy. I make sure they are well paced and move seamlessly from moment to moment. I cut needless words. I polish my sentences and make sure they are not confusing. Confuse and bore your audience, and you lose them.

Use concrete detail: Generalizations are boring and colorless. I am very specific. I draw my readers in by vividly describing the world I am creating. I don't just say "ants came down the wall." I say they came "in a black, seething river six feet wide and several inches deep."

Disasters can be opportunities: Never underestimate the storytelling possibilities of a catastrophe. Over the years, I have found that the worst things that have happened to me make the best stories.

Mary Mackey's excellent advice for creating and crafting stories is to make a personal connection, first and foremost. In storytelling, the live audience is a participant from the very beginning. The frequently inward focus of memoirists is not appropriate to a live telling. Diary-like entries can be powerful in a written essay, but often fall flat when told aloud. Mary insists that a simple story structure that begins with a catastrophe, a world turned on its head, works the very best. The worst experiences make the best stories: this is especially true for travel or adventure stories.

Crafting

Mary Mackey

Night of the Army Ants: Story Summary

In 1973, I persuaded my sister to join me on a trip to Guatemala. As we lay sleeping in a hotel in Tikal National Park, I was swarmed by army ants who came pouring through the ventilation vents and down the walls in a black, seething river six feet wide and several inches deep. I woke screaming. Thinking I was being murdered, the other guests began to pound on our door, only to discover the ants were heading their way.

The hotel staff had disappeared, the electricity was off, and there was nowhere to run except into the jungle, which was full of things far worse than ants. Retreating to the lobby, we crouched on the couches as the ants swarmed around us. Soon large scorpions began to rain down, driven out of the thatched roof by the ants. "Umbrellas!" a guy from Chicago suggested. We fled to our rooms, seized our umbrellas, opened them to keep off the scorpions, and returned to the lobby, where we sat, hunched up against one another like people waiting for a bus in a rainstorm. Occasionally a scorpion would hit one of the umbrellas, bounce to the floor, and scuttle away, but it never got far before the ants mobbed it. After two hours, we were so tired we could hardly sit upright. It was then that a man whose name I never knew, but whom neither I nor my sister will ever forget, made one of the most generous offers one human being has ever made to another: "The ants haven't made it to my room yet. If you and your sister would like to try to get some sleep in my bed, I'll hold an umbrella over you." When we woke, he was gone and so were the ants.

This story summary is a perfect example of Mary Mackey's advice: a strong voice that connects immediately to the reader, an incident of terror fraught with even more danger, and the specific details that put you in the middle of the scene. You almost feel that Mary is speaking directly to you—that she has something maddeningly delicious to tell you. Not only does Mary have an excellent voice in her work, but as a poet, she employs a skillful use of metaphor: "like people waiting for a bus in a rainstorm" is a hilarious image with a touch of the absurd. My favorite scene features the unnamed hero sitting at the side of his bed, holding the umbrella over the two sisters and himself (I hope), as scorpions fall down from their thatched roof. What tone does this story have, even in summary: tragic, comic, tragi-comic?

Trials & Challenges

Trials take the measure of us. No matter how experienced or prosperous we become, we continue to face challenges. Even if we've achieved most of our life's goals, something will come up to sorely try us. We can be thrown back on ourselves, sometimes to the core. Though trials make life difficult, they create the best stories. The appeal of any story is conflict: the more challenging, the better. We want to know how you survived, your way out, and what you learned.

One might even say that the entire purpose of the oral tradition of the ancients is to show the way out of trouble, told with an overriding belief in a positive outcome: the everlasting, happy ending. The message in most folk and fairy tales seems to be to cheer us on—urging us forward with wise advice for our journey. Kindness, compassion, honesty, humility, courage, industry, and persistence all win the day. These traditional tales see the heroic in daily life and enrich ours with meaning.

Fables, on the other hand, hope to spare us the worst and prevent catastrophe, if only we will listen. Both fables and parables are fairly simple stories with a moral lesson and share a history dating back to preliterate times. Via various storytelling customs, they were told to avert troubling or self-destructive behaviors before they could take hold in a village or a tribe.

Each of our trials teaches us a lesson through experience, one we hope to have learned well enough so as not to repeat it. Further, by shaping our experiences into tellable tales, we can share our earned wisdom through a **modern-day fable.**

These golden nuggets can be thrown into a family gathering, an everyday conversation, or a formal speech or performance.

The focus of a fable is action: what was the challenge and how did you meet it? To tell a story of trial and challenge, think of the conflict and the resolution at the same time. Think of an instance, perhaps in your youth, when you had to dig deep to deal with a situation or a crisis. We listeners need to see a struggle unfold in the rising action, your mistakes and efforts, and what you managed to learn. Perhaps it's something you wish we would all learn. Finally, articulate the moral, the universal truth in the story.

We will never forget the centuries-old impact of the Aesop's fable, "The Boy Who Cried Wolf," or the well-known children's parable, Hans Christian Anderson's "The Emperor's New Clothes." Both stories value honesty and show the dire consequences of pretense. **For your tale to be memorable, or to change a way of thinking or acting, it must be dramatic in order to prove your point. At the same time, it must be true—told in your authentic voice.**

Creating

Life offers many challenges—not all are the same size or type. Whatever a particular challenge meant to you, you faced it down and became the wiser. Whenever you tell that story, you hope to teach a life lesson or moral and empower others to avoid the same conflict and learn how to overcome it. Some trials are personal and ongoing, such as attacks against one's identity. Others are born out of external crises, perhaps financial, physical, disaster-related, or traumatic.

Personal Challenges

- Recall a time when you were personally challenged for your identity, appearance, sex, race, ethnicity, ability, or background

- Think of what happened, not simply the instance, but the entire narrative

- Reimagine the setting, the people, and the action from beginning to end

- How was the challenge resolved?

- What is the lesson or the moral?

- What do you hope will change after listeners hear your story?

The powerful stories of women's experiences that have surfaced in recent years have had a profound impact on social awareness and attitude. When any of us are finally able to tell our personal stories, we provide a platform for those who have remained silent. Many of us are survivors, not only of insults, but of assault and violence. We soon realize that the empathy that comes from sharing personal stories is often a part of our own healing journey.

Breaking the silence takes courage, but it is far better to find a safe place to speak than to remain in the shadows. As Elin Stebbins Waldal, author of *Tornado Warning: A Memoir of Teen Dating Violence and Its Effect on a Woman's Life*, so poetically states:

> "I can no longer stay quiet in this world, I have a voice and I feel it reverberate off my internal walls, making its slow climb upward until its melody can be heard all around."

Trials of Challenge & Hardship

We all have heard the meme, "When I was your age..." Here's just one example:

> "You call this snow? When I was a kid, we used to walk through snowdrifts eight feet high just to get to the woodshed."

Remarks like these cause listeners to wince and dismiss. Whenever I heard a parent or older relative make a demeaning comment like that one, trying to convince me that they and their times were tougher, I would feel diminished. Life is not a competition. Personal stories of challenge help us to understand that each one of us is a hero in our own unique journey. We can identify, empathize, and applaud one another as we walk in others' shoes. To find your story of challenge:

- Recall a time when you had to work your way out of a crisis or hardship

- During that critical time, select a few scenes that depict the problem and its challenging tasks

- Allow us to experience the challenge with you through sensory images and key details

- Keep to the main action

- How was the crisis resolved?

- What did you learn?

- How do you hope to change your listeners by telling this story?

Avoid "telling" listeners the meaning you made of the challenge. If you weigh down your hardship story with commentary, they will not be able to experience the lesson and learn it vicariously. For example, the following passage is all commentary with no story elements, and it falls flat. What could have the potential for a powerful story of challenge is simply informative prose:

> When I was a kid, we moved all the time, at least once a year, maybe more. I never had a stable home or school and always had to make new friends. Sometimes all I owned fit in a child's suitcase—with my toys and books left behind. I learned how to do with little and adapt to new places.

Compare it to an action story of challenge, one that was indeed formative, but told as the incident unfolded:

> **Cupertino, CA 1960**
>
> "Starting up!" The guy on the high platform yelled loud enough for every worker in the barn-sized workhouse to hear. He turned on the conveyor belt with a clank and a lurch and dumped the first crate of apricots through an array of sprinklers—fresh off the orchard trees just outside the canning shed doors.
>
> As a jumbled heap of apricots rolled toward me, the first station on the belt, I clenched my paring knife in one hand and used the other to sort through the fruit. Scanning the mess, I grabbed twigs, leaves, green 'cots, and other debris

that went into a bucket on my left side, and I looked for rotten fruit that went into a bucket on my right side, along with any brown or bruised spots I trimmed with my knife.

That first day on the job, there were about fifteen workers stationed along the catwalk on either side of the belt. Bent to the never-ending blur of 'cots with a steady focus, I still noticed a tall, dark man with a pencil-thin mustache wearing well-pressed khakis slink behind us on the narrow ledge.

The second day, there were only seven of us. Unknown to me, a rookie at seasonal canning jobs, the foreman and floor lady had watched for speed and accuracy and kept the fastest workers. At the morning break, I learned about that drill from my Latina coworkers. The only Anglo on the belt, and the only English speaker, I was proud I'd passed the test against more experienced help. I retied my splattered, plastic bib apron, ready to prove my worth again and earn the much-needed tuition for my sophomore year in college.

The third day, I woke with every muscle aching and rashes on my arms from the acidic fruit. The thought of facing that endless stream of apricots was almost unbearable.

My mother stood in the bedroom door, knowing it was past time for me to rise. "It'll be harder to get up tomorrow," she said, in a flat tone.

Not needing another prompt, I raced to get ready; I grabbed my cleaned plastic apron and began the mile-long walk to the canning shed. I crossed Stevens Creek Road, and soon I was running down the gravel lane through the orchards, breathless. When the corrugated aluminum shed appeared through the leafy groves, I saw the floor lady outside the barn doors, waiting for me.

"I wondered if you'd come today," she said, smiling, and handed me my timecard to clock in.

The fourth day, I was on the catwalk on time, ready to work. Just before the conveyor belt started up, I saw a Portuguese woman next to me make the sign of the cross. She told me that her work was a prayer. Humbled, I was never late to the canning shed again that summer.

When the last apricot crate was picked and canned, the job was over.

The ladies on the line asked me, "¿Vas a Libby's?"

I would've liked to work the tomato crop at Libby's Cannery in Sunnyvale, but it was too far from Cupertino. My heart swelled with pride because they'd asked me, included me as a *comadre* in the harsh cycle of seasonal canning. I'd made rank!

The apricot orchards in Cupertino are long gone; where the canning shed stood is now Apple Park, world headquarters of Apple, Inc. But those long summer days on the conveyor belt gave me more than an hourly wage: I learned the sustaining power of hard work—and that I could trust myself to do it.

But I never acquired a taste for apricots.

Crafting

To shape this story, I began in the middle of the action, inside the canning shed in a fast-moving workplace. Even though my parents had warned me that I could not return to college unless I earned my tuition that summer, I embedded that urgent motive later in the narrative. My first challenge was to learn how to keep a physically demanding job. I also decided to use a simple story structure, numbering my days on the job: one, two, three, four. Odds were I wouldn't last, so each day was a milestone. The countdown structure also made it easier to tell the story by heart.

Because so much of our past intersects with history in our rapidly changing society, I wanted to place my summer story in the shifting context of the San Francisco Bay Area's storied past. The transformation couldn't be more dramatic: Santa Clara Valley, home to hundreds of fruit orchards, became the world-famous Silicon Valley—from luscious fruit trees with fragrant blossoms and delicious crops to brittle microchips and digital devices that propel global technologies.

In my research, I found that Spaniards planted the first apricot trees in Mission Santa Clara back in the 1700s; by 1919, there were millions of fruit trees in the valley and 665,000 apricot trees. But by 1960, orchards were bulldozed to make way for tract home developments due to the rapid rise in California's post-war population. One book, *California Apricots: The Lost Orchards of Silicon Valley*, laments the fact that Santa Clara Valley was once the largest apricot producer in the world and remembers it with nostalgic stories of its lost orchards.

As a teen, I had no idea that the job that challenged me in 1960 was already vanishing. Yet my path that summer crisscrossed the changing divide: I'd walked to work from a new tract home, crossing both a main road and into another era. At mid-century, the valley was a checkerboard of competing economies.

This historical context helped me to understand the economic forces that allowed me to participate in this unlikely summer job. It made it more real, grounded, and possible, and it validated my daily traverse from a suburban development to a rural orchard.

Layers of Meaning

When you select and craft a story of challenge or hardship, you'll soon discover it has elements that are not readily apparent. It is after all a significant tale, one with profound personal meaning. As you consider sharing your story with others, uncover other aspects within it. This will deepen your understanding of its meaning with the potential to change you and others. In selecting this challenge story from my teen years, "Cupertino, CA 1960," I discovered it was consequential for many reasons:

- It takes place in the California *boom* years, the vast migration of the fifties and sixties

- Cultural/class crossover—my taking a migrant's job

- Introduction to following seasonal crops

- Intersection of suburban and rural communities

- Transition for me from the Latinx city of San Antonio, TX, to white, suburban Cupertino, CA

- Trial by fire introduction to the physical demands of manual labor

- Increased understanding of Spanish and Portuguese languages

- Value of a union shop organized by Teamsters

Not only was I learning my own lessons of persistence and the intrinsic value of hard work, I was perched on the edge of what would become full-blown cultural and political confrontations throughout the sixties and seventies: farm workers' strikes, teen runaways from affluent suburbs, the counterculture revolution, and the advent of mass political protests. Finally, there would be the incredible irony of the Apple tech empire burgeoning in the middle of centuries-old fruit orchards in the early nineties—the start of the tech revolution. Fertile ground, indeed, for real and digital fruit.

All of these threads are part of the raw material interwoven in your personal stories. They are the connections of the personal to history, to culture, to society. **As you spin your tales of challenge, you will find them inevitably linked to a larger society and its history.**

Telling

When you begin to understand the significance of your tale of challenge, both for yourself and for others who've faced a similar challenge, your sense of its meaning will deepen. As this occurs, you'll find yourself telling it in different settings or to achieve a specific purpose, such as increased social awareness.

As you review the sequence of events in your story, jot them down in a simple outline, noting key words and images. In this way, you'll be able to tell the story in a new way each time without memorizing a script. You'll adapt the story to a variety of situations and make it compelling each time.

Outline the story, stripping details down to keywords and indicating its narrative arc. Keep the outline of a story in a story journal, on index cards, or by using a storyboard.

1. Setting: automated canning shed, apricot orchard, Cupertino, CA, 1960

2.   Characters: Me, migrant workers, foreman, floor lady

3.   First day: fifteen workers on the conveyor belt, sorting apricots

4.   Second day: seven most efficient workers selected— only one Anglo

5.   Third day: sore, aching, rash, reluctant to return, mother's advice, arrived late

6.   Fourth day: motivated, on time, humbled

7.   Fifth scene: end of apricot crop

8.   Sixth scene: accepted as a *comadre*

9.   Resolution: sustaining power of hard work, trustworthiness

In Chapter Four, you'll discover more tools for displaying the elements of your story, such as a story map or storyboard. You'll also find techniques for delivery.

The "Seven Steps to Storytelling" were original to the Word Weaving Storytelling Project and featured throughout its highly successful trainings for educators. These demystify the art of storytelling into easy-to-learn steps.

Exercises & Prompts: Trials & Challenges

Prompts: Personal Challenge

Select challenging incidents that were resolved in some basic way so that others can learn from them, either through an astute reflection, a lesson, or the moral of the story.

Private Setting

1. Was there a time in your private life when you were in danger?

2. Did you ever feel your personhood was under attack from family, friends, or associates?

3. Did you fear for your safety in your personal relationships?

4. Did you experience trauma in your home life?

5. **How did you resolve these situations, and what did you learn or what would you like listeners to learn from them?**

Public Setting

1. Was there a time when you were confronted, insulted, or attacked in public or at work?

2. Was there an instance in a public space where you felt vulnerable and afraid, yet escaped—a close call?

3. Think of a time when you were belittled or shamed in public.

4. Was there an incident when you felt discriminated against?

5. **How did you resolve these situations, and what did you learn or what would you like listeners to learn from them?**

Prompts: Challenge of Crisis or Hardship

1. Was there a time when your well-being was at stake?

2. Did you have to dig deep at some point in your life to succeed?

3. How did you survive a crisis? A disaster?

4. Have you experienced a period of ongoing crisis?

5. **How did you resolve these situations, and what did you learn or what would you like listeners to learn from them?**

Storytellers Share Secrets: Trials & Challenges

In contemporary society, many stories of personal challenges that were once suffered in silence are now being told. Often these are hard to hear, and sometimes they can create a backlash. In previous decades, for example, personal accounts of domestic violence, sexual assault, or childhood abuse were systemically repressed. Breaking the silence takes courage, yet all can learn from another's experiences of abuse. If we are able to share our stories of pain and personal trials openly and responsibly, we can help create a more empathetic community.

These two storytellers share unique yet similar incidents. Reading them has the potential to change our behavior while releasing the pain of the experience itself through the telling.

Creating

Michel Wing identifies as a nonbinary, disabled writer who lives and works in New Mexico. They have spent the bulk of their life working on visibility on issues such as domestic violence awareness, disability rights, sexual assault prevention, and LGBTQI advocacy. Their publications include *Body on the Wall* (poems) and *Cry of the Nightbird: Writers Speak Against Domestic Violence* (as coeditor), both under the name of Michelle Wing. Their poetry and essays have also been anthologized widely. *Note: Michel uses* they *and* their *instead of he/she and his/her in third person pronouns so as to avoid being categorized by gender.*

My Storytelling Process

Michel Wing

When I think of a story, I imagine it in my mind as it happened. I remember the setting, the characters, the dialogue, the movement—how it happened from beginning to end. Then I try to create a frame for the story to hold it all together and give it an arc or theme. Almost always, something emerges. There will be a little clue at the beginning that points to the end, or the opposite of that:

a beginning that makes the end surprising. There may be something that makes the reader feel safe, and then the end wallops you. But if you don't pay attention, if you leave out that little moment, the story will be incomplete.

Most importantly, though, when I tell a story, I am a truth teller. I make sure what I say is real and honest. There are no made-up parts. I often tell hard stories, because there are some people who are unable to tell their own stories for various reasons. I can. And I want to do it right.

We can change minds and hearts with our stories. That is power. I won't abuse it.

It's clear from the advocacy work Michel Wing has undertaken over the years that their stories seek to make a difference, to create a vicarious experience in both poetry and prose. They would like you to see the world through their eyes, and by so doing, shift your perspective.

Crafting

The Hat

Michel Wing

I had a negative encounter in my hometown of Las Cruces, New Mexico, that left me cold.

I went to lunch at a restaurant with a new, young friend to get to know her better. Rick, our waiter, was great. The waiter who brought our food was also great—a young gay man who wears makeup. He remembered me from a previous visit and greeted me warmly. We ate, paid, and stayed to chat for a bit. And then, there was the incident.

I happened to be wearing a hat with an LGBT logo on it, something I hadn't even thought about when leaving the house. Black ball cap, big logo. As my friend and I talked, the man at the booth behind us stood up to leave. He unfolded himself into the aisle, a tall silver-haired man, placing a military veteran's ball cap on his head as he stood. I noticed all of this because he stared at me piercingly the entire time. Just as he reached his full height, adjusting his own cap, he stepped right beside me and said, "Nice hat."

It was not the words. It was the tone, the facial expression, the body language, the posture. It was everything. He walked away. I said to my friend, "That didn't feel good." She said, "No. No, it didn't feel good at all."

I haven't felt that kind of open hostility in some time. It was like an ice dagger in my chest.

Hate hurts.

This story is difficult to hear, partly because Michel is a skillful writer. Michel frames the incident in the role of an eyewitness, and that makes it more effective than an emotional venting or rant. We watch the action unfold, though it is framed by the sensory images of cold and ice at beginning and end. That such pain can be inflicted so easily, so randomly, is the terror that walks in our society. A midday lunch in a welcoming diner, one where Michel had eaten before, did not prepare them for this personal attack. What part of the story did you find most effective? How did this story affect you?

Creating

Lisa Bishop, MLIS, is a graduate of the San Jose State University School of Library and Information Science—part of a groundbreaking group of teachers reinvigorating the SFUSD school library program. She is a member of ALA and AASL and a conference presenter. She is also active in the book arts community and encourages students to write their own stories and enter them into the Ezra Jack Keats Bookmaking Competition, where her students have won many prizes. When asked to contribute a story of personal challenge, Lisa wrote that this one "hit her over the head."

Crafting

Are You There God? It's Me, Hussy

Lisa Bishop

"Psssssst, girls, over here. Do you want a job?" Her face protruded from the carryout window of the local diner in our small town of Plymouth, Michigan. She wiggled her forefinger, beckoning. She offered my best friend Vanessa and me a dollar an hour, good pay back in 1976.

One weekend, after being hired at the diner, I went to the famous J.L. Hudson department store's annual sale and discovered the bargain bra bin. I bought a new style of bra that today we call a "sports bra": one piece, with no hooks, no pads, no strap, nor any underwire digs. *It felt great*. Of course I wore it to my new job. My uniform consisted of a white cotton blouse, black pants, and a full front apron.

I heard my boss, Alice, behind me hiss, "You look like a hussy!"

Hussy? I hadn't heard that term before, but I knew it wasn't complimentary. It sounded like a slut or a whore, words I *had* heard before. I couldn't understand how anyone would even notice my new bra with my apron covering my blouse. But the sting of Alice's insult, with her pointy face and her backcombed, sprayed hair, has stayed with me my entire life.

Boobs were a big deal in middle school. In sixth grade, a few of us read Judy Blume's novel *Are You There God? It's Me, Margaret*, and formed an "itty bitty titty committee" like the characters in the book: "We must, we must, we must increase our bust, the bigger the better, the tighter the sweater—the boys depend on us."

I currently teach middle school. I'm very sensitive to the body image pressures on young girls. I am aware of how I speak to these impressionable young women and know that **words do hurt**.

The word *hussy* even sounds sinister. That it was an unknown, archaic word to this young teen made it even more so—in the way Lisa freely associated *hussy* with other, more damaging words. It triggered many self-doubts at a vulnerable age, the onslaught of puberty, when sexual identity is newly forming. That the insult remained with Lisa throughout her life is an indication of how shocking and painful it was to her person— worse than a slap.

Back then, Lisa found comic relief in the perennially popular book she mentions, Judy Blume's young adult fiction tale of a teen girl with "itty, bitty, titties" with whom Lisa and her friends identify. Lisa echoed this fictional connection in the title of her story. Doing so frames the story within the wider context of the preoccupations of teen girls. It is a plea for sensitivity to girls' adolescent physical development during its most tender phase. *"Are you there—for them?"* Lisa asks through the title's analogy. It comes as no surprise that Lisa is a school librarian who promotes literacy, books, and students' stories in her middle school library.

Motifs in Storytelling

Both these stories are set in the **all-American diner**, in what should be a safe space—an extended living room in any community. "Where friends meet friends" is a common motto for a neighborhood diner. It's remarkable to me that while neither storyteller, Michel Wing nor Lisa Bishop, knows of the other's work and while they live in different time zones, they repeated similar patterns: the diner setting, a random insult, and a similar moral concerning personal pain.

This phenomenon of the motif often occurs in the oral tradition: repeated elements in tales from far-flung cultures. A motif has significance when repeated, taking on a symbolic meaning that connects to the "big idea" in the story. In these two stories, we see an acute awareness of something our culture is slowly coming to understand: what might have once been acceptable can no longer be tolerated. Catcalls in the street and cutting insults hurled at those with differences all have consequences. The hashtag movements on social media and the many personal stories told on digital platforms have brought a greater sensitivity to our everyday interactions.

Both Michel and Lisa want us to hear and feel the insults spoken in a shared community space and to internalize them. Each wrote a similar moral at the end of their story in almost the exact words: **Hate hurts; words do hurt.** This is a message essential enough to have been shared spontaneously in two separate submissions, a message that makes these two personal stories modern-day fables for our time.

There are universal patterns in the worldwide oral tradition, which is something that no one can truly explain. In Chapter Five, we'll take another look at motifs and other elements within the common heritage of folklore. You may be surprised to find story motifs or even archetypes in your own original tales.

Creating

Lee Goff is the author of the Thunder Trilogy, a businessman, business owner, husband, father, grandfather, and friend. He is formally educated, having received undergraduate degrees in both English and finance and one graduate degree. Lee is the son of a career military officer; he grew up in a household considered normal at the time with a loving mother and father.

Lee Goff

Stories have been used since human beings first sat around a campfire, usually for the purpose of teaching something, whether it be a warning, a moral, or giving a past act a legacy. At some point, a man or woman set on making an impact began a story with, "Let me tell you about the time I..." And from there, the listener either embraced the lesson or denied it. In either case, the storyteller had a responsibility; the story contained a purpose. Before writing any short story or novel, I ask myself, "What am I trying to convey?" And from there, I practice the very proactive and intentional avoidance of any attempt at making the reader feel the way I did. It's my responsibility to write a story, make it believable and relevant, then let the reader's emotional chips fall where they may. If the reader comes away from it in a thoughtful manner, then I've succeeded in my purpose, which is to entertain—to allow a reader the luxury, if only for a short time, of an escape from whatever he or she needs to escape from.

Lee Goff shows his respect for message over teller in how he selects a story. His creative sense of the art is similar to that of traditional storytellers, who let go of their egos so the story can take center stage. For example, when the ancient troubadour picked up his or her harp or lyre to recite or sing a tale many had heard before, she or he was not the focus. Like black-robed musicians in a symphony orchestra, the teller was invisible, while the story filled the great halls with its compelling reality. Each listener identified with it as he felt moved. This objective, hands-off method seems antithetical to contemporary storytellers who want us to empathize directly with their experiences. Yet both styles of storytelling can be equally effective. Once the framework and the sequence of action are set, the narrator can assume a neutral role so that the story itself can have a powerful impact. It's clear that Lee's stories are chosen for a lesson and with a purpose—they are relevant and unforgettable. This is the traditional way of telling.

Crafting

Zero Entitlement: Story Summary

Lee Goff

"Mr. Goff, you haven't learned a thing. You sincerely feel you're better than everyone else." The judge banged her gavel, looked at me, and spoke. "Mr. Goff, welcome to the Texas Prison System. Probation revoked."

The air may have left the room at that point, but I wouldn't have noticed it; I was too terrified to breathe. My innocence was irrelevant.

What is relevant is when a man walks through life, he feels like he's in control, that he's brave, that he can face anything, and worse: he's part of a business and social circle that is "untouchable." To say I was afraid was an understatement; the fact is, I was terrified. But life teaches men not to show fear, and understanding enough about human nature to know that predators prey on the weak, I realized I had to show the hard shell, saying little, confronting no one, avoiding conflict.

It was in prison that I found freedom. I listened to life stories, confessing to myself that I'd judged men unfairly, that my arrogance and entitlement were traits that made me less of a good man than many of the men I met behind bars. I found that kindness could be a strength; once I began tutoring men for their GED, helping them with legal work, and editing their letters home, regardless of race or background, I found a group of men grateful to me. I was told I was the first white man who had treated them with respect. I found that my simple acts of assistance bridged chasms between me and them.

It was in my hell that I found my heaven. It was in the darkness that I found the light in every man. It was in my status as a convict that I found the best man I could be. And in all of this, I found I could face anything.

True to his self-effacing storytelling style, Lee Goff seeks in this tale to resolve the age-old conflict of arrogance versus compassion. That clash is emphatically set in motion with the bang of a gavel wielded by a female judge. Lee narrates a situation of great challenge, a trial that ultimately strips away his veneer of privilege. That he is able to use the benefits of his background and share them with other inmates is both a tribute to him and his way out. He not only survived the ordeal but was empowered by it. These are the classic elements of a folktale: the hero's journey through danger and his triumph.

According to Joseph Campbell, the final stage in the hero's journey is that he returns home a changed man. He has grown as a person, learned many things, faced many terrible dangers and even death, but now looks forward to the start of a new life. The final reward may be either literal or an inner achievement—whatever it is, it represents three things: change, success, and proof of the impact of his journey. The hero returns to where he started, but things will never be the same again.

So it is that contemporary personal stories echo the themes and truths of the ancient tales. This is particularly true of stories of hardship and challenge.

Spun Gold

In this chapter, we've demonstrated how to pull together the raw stuff of experience and spin it into powerful stories. Several contributors and I have shared secrets of how to select, create, and craft compelling personal stories around a few themes. As you make the storytelling art your own, you'll experiment with our techniques and find your own methods or create a combination.

The three themes modeled in this chapter are frequently selected for personal tales, but there are many other thought-provoking and entertaining topics. For example, schooling is one that can immediately evoke conflict, humor, and tension, along with memorable characters and situations.

Though we've followed the storytelling art from a raw idea to a narrative shape through a variety of means, we've kept to the basic elements that make up every successful story:

- **Setting**
- **Characters**
- **Conflict, tension**
- **Narrative arc of rising action, increasing tension**
- **Sensory images within the action**
- **Dialogue within the action**
- **Resolution of conflict**

In addition, we've modeled doing some research and finding layers of meaning within each curated tale. This is the critical weave in the telling, one that changes you and the listener.

The more you can tell without saying, the more impact your story will have. In theater, this is the subtext; in written memoir, it's the commentary of the author. In the live, oral art of storytelling, the complexity of deeper meanings in your story is delivered with tone, mood, voice, gesture, and emotion.

We have woven the first threads in the storytelling process through creating and crafting, but the real magic takes place in a live telling. Certainly, you will have changed as you focused on your life experiences in a written piece, a journal entry, a free write draft, story outline, or storyboard. When you select and shape your stories, you create them in an intensive framework and learn more about yourself and the core lessons of your life.

But the storytelling alchemy is complete only when you tell your story aloud. That is when the transformation takes place: Telling your story to a live audience, even in a private conversation, is the point of maximum change. Not only do you contribute to social discourse by sharing wisdom—honoring the personal over mass media, and the live connection over the digital—but you produce a dynamic dialogue with a live audience. At some point, you are all telling the story together, adding meaning and dimension to it: an ever-changing tapestry.

Chapter Two

Stuff We Are Made Of

We are such stuff As dreams are made on,
and our little life Is rounded with a sleep.

—*The Tempest*, Act IV, Shakespeare

Introduction

It seems we are always getting to know ourselves throughout the many stages of our lives. Yet we are often confused by both the way others perceive us and the onslaught of media images and cultural expectations in conflict with our own. What is the "stuff" that is unique to us, and how do we find our true nature in spite of outside influences? We may surprise ourselves with spontaneous acts of courage or defeat ourselves with consuming fear; we may at times dismay our friends with our mistakes, or we might rise to an occasion with brilliant success. Each time, we have a hint of the inner stuff which we are made of.

Social media provides a platform for us to display aspects of our lives, opinions, and achievements. But these seem to fragment us into bite-sized pieces in a constant feed of posts, images, and chats. Rather than offering us an opportunity to express ourselves in some authentic way, it often adds to our veneer—to the surface shine in a media mirror. We only post what we want others to see: our best day, best meal out, a charming weekend in Paris, or an immediate crisis.

You can come to know yourself through the art of storytelling, if you are paying attention. If you are the unseen eyewitness to your own actions, you will recognize yourself through your choices, trials, challenges, joys, and outcomes. Imagine you had a self-driving car with a dash cam capturing your life journey. What would it record in the encounters that matter? How would you come across? With unflinching honesty, you can begin to appreciate and accept the person you are in your actions and interactions by recording your everyday stories.

Self-reflection is essential in knowing yourself, away from the daily pressures of expectation and conformity. One proven way is the practice of journaling. I took up the habit of journaling because I often found myself outside the norm: I felt the urge to explain myself to myself.

- How and why did the latest crisis happen?
- Why didn't I compromise?
- Why do I take risks?
- What is driving me?

Over time, while reading and rereading journal passages, flagging some and highlighting others, patterns emerged. I came to learn about myself: the conflicts within me, those I faced in society and in my own character—and what I was most likely to do in the future. The need for articulate self-explanation through the writing process is not only my own. **The emerging genre of memoir is a growing trend, with more published every year.** No longer is the autobiography the exclusive territory of a celebrity working with a ghost writer. Memoirs are written by ordinary people whose skill and insight plumb the depths of experience to share their journey, exposing the pivotal roles of personal choice and character.

Storytelling and personal narrative have also gained significant value in the marketplace. Authentic stories about a product or service seem to restore a human connection; they feel deeper than the hype and can be unforgettable. A brand story is not just a catchy tagline or ad jingle that gets stuck in your head. It differs from traditional stories in that it requires reasoning or a "why" story that connects the audience emotionally with the product or person. Branding experts say that the story of any product can be so powerful that consumers are tempted to consider a purchase.

So personal stories remain an unavoidable and important part of our culture's storehouse of knowledge: they communicate meaningful information in a genuine way. In spite of that, mainstream media tends to focus on the surface images and descriptions that polarize us. If we view ourselves through the lens of those various facets, we can find ourselves distracted and bewildered. There are endless ways to portray ourselves: height, weight, gender and/or sexual identity, ethnicity, race, place of origin, religion, political affiliation, education, income, and favorite ice cream flavor.

None of these superficial descriptions tell your story— the through line to your core identity. Regardless of all the billions of people who share this planet, not one has your fingerprints; not one has your unique gifts or your story to tell.

How do you go about creating your defining story, a signature story, a branding story? In this chapter, we'll take the plunge into that raw material—that stuff—to discover the most telling tales. The stories we create are meant to be told to a live audience, shared in conversation, or related in a public talk. This live exchange will heighten the meaning of each story as it resonates with listeners. **It is in sharing our authentic selves through story that our social discourse can find stability—our common ground.**

Defining Story

This above all: to thine own self be true And it must follow,
as the night the day Thou canst not then be false to any man.

—*Hamlet,* Act I, Shakespeare

Defining stories are at the heart of self-discovery.
They have the power to express our unique identity to others.
Circumstances bring out the best and worst in us, but more
importantly, they expose our true natures. We see ourselves
cast on life's stage with the spotlight trained on our choices
and actions in a pivotal scene. It could be a moment of choice
or challenge, but whatever caused intensity in a given event, it
pushed us to the core and defined us. Look for a time when you
stepped up, front and center, and took a stand. In that incident,
you became more visible, lit by personal motivations and
passions—even during your earliest years.

For example, when I was about ten, living in the Southside area
of San Antonio, Texas, in a modest neighborhood, I decided to
put on a play at my house. I asked my best friend, Janie, to be
in it, but she declined. Annoyed by her betrayal, I pushed on,
and I convinced my five-year-old brother to learn Janie's part.
I tacked signs on telephone poles announcing the performance.
A small crowd gathered, but my brother was overcome with
stage fright and hid under the covers in the bedroom. I had to
take all the parts myself.

This important memory was at first clouded by my failures:
that my best friend wouldn't participate and that my brother
hid under the covers. But on reflection, I finally had to admit

that I was coming out as a storyteller and producer. My original script, based on fairy-tale books borrowed from the library, grew from a childhood desire to share the tales I found most fascinating. That I was motivated to perform them in an unlikely neighborhood without urging or encouragement was an authentic expression of who I was. As a through line in my life's work, that early event was clearly a defining one.

It's often true that we begin to know our innate gifts and proclivities in late childhood, a time when we are relatively free to explore before peer pressure sets in. It's a fertile phase of life for self-discovery and development. Nevertheless, we are daily confronted with who we are as we mature. We continue to develop as adults, and we increase our capacities in many ways beyond mere survival. In fulfilling our potential, we are most likely to encounter ourselves in those interactions and experiences that are most nurturing—in our bliss.

Creating

How do you capture that slippery sense of self in a defining story? Think of the lasting impressions that came to mind when you looked for defining life situations in your past to help you know yourself better. Imagine yourself at the center of a whirlwind of memories: instances of achievement, praiseworthy occasions, and moments of supreme self-satisfaction. Isolate times of self-expression or those of constant preoccupation. Imagine introducing yourself to someone who wants to know who you are, not what you do. Most people might want to immediately categorize you by externals, and they might miss the essentials. You can avoid this by sharing your defining stories.

For a defining story to hold your listeners' attention and have an impact, it needs to have the entire complement of an unforgettable tale:

- Setting: Where did it take place?

- Conflict: What was the essential problem, crisis, disagreement, or challenge?

- Action: What are the scenes in the story? What is the rising action?

- Who are the real-life characters?

- What is the dialogue?

- Finally, what is the reveal? What did you learn about your identity that you didn't know?

If you can't answer all these questions with distinctive content, then your memory is not a story, but a brief vignette or anecdote.

For example, as I began to construct events from my self-revealing memories, one vivid recollection came to mind:

When I was in the seventh grade at a Catholic elementary school, one of the nuns cast me in the role of a Native American crone, an old woman in fake buckskin who had a long soliloquy in the school play. The day of the performance, I sat cross-legged on a rise in the middle of the auditorium, not on the stage, and recited all my lines perfectly, rhythmically, as if it were a familiar occurrence.

This was certainly a significant memory in light of my lifelong interest in storytelling. I remember wondering why I was chosen to be the crone, what that meant about me as a young girl. But as hard as I tried, I could not remember further details. The performance seemed dreamlike, surreal, yet I know it took place. What I understood at the time was that the nun must have known I would memorize my lines and that I would rise to the occasion. Now I see she also understood something about my nature: that I had a certain presence, a willingness to be seen as older or wiser, and the ability to play an unusual part for my age with conviction. However, this was not a defining story, but only a glimpse into self.

Compare it to another memory from much later in life that was crystal clear in my mind, with lights, camera, and action. This was such a vivid incident; it was one that was not only pivotal but revealing. **I learned something about myself I did not consciously understand until that day.** Until the year before this occurrence, a year in which I'd become a mother, I'd considered myself a dilettante—someone with talent and some charm, but one who dabbled in the arts. Even after receiving an impressive grant from a prestigious foundation, I'd suffered from imposter syndrome. Primal as it was, motherhood did not allow me such frivolities. I began to take myself and my talents seriously, since I was soon to depend on them for survival.

One year after my son's birth, I was on my own just as the three-year period of a storytelling grant was to end. For reasons difficult to understand, my son's father could not cope with a newborn. I sought safety for myself and my son by leaving and rented a room from a savvy landlord in a nearby community. While I watched my savings dwindle each day and as I completed the last work of the grant, I developed a new storytelling proposal and was soon given an opportunity to pitch it to the entire board of trustees at one time. I was to propose a statewide project in partnership with the California Department of Education.

Sea Cliff 1983

"Wait just a hot minute," my housemate said. "I'm getting ready to launch you!"

I hesitated on the front porch of the East Bay bungalow. "Just *what* are you doing?"

My African American landlord was laying strings of firecrackers on each side of the front yard's sidewalk. "It's your send-off." He put a match to the fuses, and the firecrackers began to pop. Smoke filled the air. "Walk through! This is your big day." He yelled over the racket.

Feeling like I was being shot from a cannon, I dashed through the smoky sidewalk in my high heels and turned and waved as I reached the street. We shared big grins, a show of bravado. Somewhat shaky after the noise and smoke, I found my car and prepared to drive to a swanky reception in the City that would make or break me.

I wore my only nice dress, a silk shirtdress my mother had sewn before I was pregnant, a soft shade of beige with a discreet floral pattern, appropriate for that warm spring afternoon. Now with my son one year old, it easily fit, even belted. It was for him that this meeting had to go well. I was his sole support.

As I approached the freeway, I hoped my used, battered car, not always dependable, would make it over the Bay Bridge to the exclusive Sea Cliff neighborhood in San Francisco. I rehearsed my remarks on the way and the story I planned to tell. All the foundation executives and the board of trustees would be there to hear selected grant recipients give oral reports. My goal was to extend my funding with a story. It was a bold move.

I'd chosen the story carefully: it depicted a great and magical Chinese dragon that appeared as an older, paunchy, bald man—similar to many of the foundation's wealthy executives. I would surprise them all with my audacious storytelling and then propose a statewide project—in a cold pitch.

At last, on the winding streets of Sea Cliff, perched on the northern bluffs of the city, I parked my car a few blocks away, out of sight, and walked to the opulent home of the philanthropist. A maid answered the door in full uniform: a black dress with a stiff white apron and cap.

I entered a stunning parlor with tall windows that looked out to the Golden Gate and the Marin Headlands; it was sumptuous, filled with wondrous antiques, black lacquered floor screens, plush armchairs, and settees on Persian carpets. Maids circulated with silver trays and dainty hors d'oeuvres. Lavish bouquets of spring flowers filled porcelain vases. We honorees were told to speak in front of the grand piano, which the chairs faced.

One of the foundation assistants approached me, saying, "You're wearing the only dress that matches this room. So elegant." I thought, *Wasn't that lucky?*

My presentation was a blur of words; I remember gesturing wildly. But the gaggle of older guys standing at the back of the room got the joke. They roared when the bald old man in the story transformed into the Great Cloud Dragon.

As I was leaving, the executive director beckoned me with a wry smile. "I just found out I'm funding a statewide, storytelling project."

Amazed, I shook his hand. They'd already agreed among themselves, just like that. I sailed over the Bay Bridge back to the East Bay to pick up my darling child from the babysitter. We would survive and thrive—all because of stories.

Later, I wondered: would I have dared to take on the millionaires if I weren't a mother?

Crafting

In crafting this story, I began with a moment of drama: the fireworks! The immediate contrast between my lowly, rented room over a cottage's garage to the mansion in Sea Cliff was a striking setting for the main action. **This was the kind of high-stakes situation that would most likely reveal a basic quality of a person—a deeper sense of who I was and what I could be.** What I learned was that a greater sense of responsibility gave me more authority as well as increased motivation. As a new mother, I challenged myself to provide for my child and to mature as an adult, fulfilling my own potential.

To make certain my memory served me correctly, I searched at the public library for the story I told, *Everyone Knows What a Dragon Looks Like* by Jay Williams and illustrated by Mercer Mayer (1976).

In the story, the poor street sweeper, Han, greets a fat, little, old man at the gate to the city of Wu. When the old man claims to be the Great Cloud Dragon that all have beseeched to save the city from the Wild Horsemen of the North, Han says he doesn't think the old man looks like a dragon. And neither does anyone else in the city: not the Mandarin, the Captain of the Army, the Chief of the Workmen, the Leader of the Merchants, nor the Wisest of the Wise Men. They dismiss the old man and refuse to treat him with courtesy.

It is only Han, the orphaned street sweeper, who welcomes the little, fat, bald, old man into his hut and serves him a cup of wine and a bowl of rice. Because of that courtesy, the Great Cloud Dragon sends fierce winds, lightning, and terrifying storms against the approaching Wild Horsemen, who flee. And only then does the fat little man reveal himself as a dragon, filling the sky with a roar and with his huge body, his scales the color of sunset clouds, his claws and teeth glittering like diamonds.

Researching the story and reading it again facilitated my memories of that day, the emotions, and the underlying humor of the occasion.

Layers of Meaning

As you select and craft a story worthy of telling—a defining story—you'll notice there are elements and layers within it that might not be apparent at first. In the example story, "Sea Cliff 1983," there were many unique layers—those I knew or communicated between the lines:

- Renewed commitment to the art of storytelling

- Defined myself as a storyteller on a larger stage

- Exhibited the survival instincts of motherhood

- Demonstrated the power of story as a marketing tool

- Internalized the dragon story to see a power beyond outward trappings

- Appreciated the opportunities of the entrepreneurial spirit in the SF Bay Area

- Valued the support of the Jewish philanthropic community

Though the elderly philanthropists at the foundation's reception enjoyed identifying themselves with a magical, mythical beast as they heard the dragon story, they also appreciated its moral: we are all more than our outward appearance, and each of us has a brilliance, a gift. Perhaps we all need a Han, an orphan boy with no pretensions, to honor us with courtesy, a cup of tea, and a bowl of rice, to coax us out— so that we can be seen for who we truly are.

Telling

A defining story is one that is powerful in relation to the teller's identity and is based on self-reflection. How you continue to understand its pivotal meaning in your life will influence how and when you tell it to others.

When you have created a rough draft of a defining story, simplify its sequence of events into an outline. Once the story is reduced to key words and images that trigger other details in the story, you'll be able to tell it freely without needing to memorize.

Outline the story, stripping details down to keywords and indicating its narrative arc.

For example, here is an outline of "Sea Cliff 1983":

1. Setting: East Bay bungalow to San Francisco mansion

2. Characters: Landlord, reception guests, executive director, me

3. First scene: Send-off with fireworks in East Bay; conflict, high stakes

4. Second scene: Drive & arrival at Sea Cliff; rising tension

5. Third scene: Presentation, storytelling; rising action

6. Resolution: Success, received funding

7. Conclusion: Return to pick up son, new sense of motherhood and the power of story

Keep the outline of a story in a story journal, on index cards, or by using a storyboard.

With your story outlined, refer to Chapter Four to find other tools, such as graphic organizers. A storyboard is particularly effective since it includes both key words and images.

The "Seven Steps to Storytelling" were original to the Word Weaving Storytelling Project and featured throughout its highly successful, professional trainings for educators. These demystify the art of storytelling into easy-to-learn steps.

Exercises & Prompts: Signature Story

Storyline: Timeline

1. Think of a year when you began to have a self-concept separate from others' expectations

2. During that year, any year, remember a time when you had a new sense of self

3. Jot down qualities of self you observed over the years and link each to an event

4. Think of a time when you surprised yourself with an unknown ability

5. Consider drawing a self-discovery timeline, from your earliest years to the present

6. For each significant point in the timeline, describe the key event and what you came to know about yourself

7. Create a word cloud, mind map, or list of all the qualities that define your essential self

8. Select your most central, defining quality and match it to an incident

9. Frame the key event into a narrative arc

Follow the Documents

1. Recall the major documents throughout your life: certificates, degrees, awards, trophies

2. Gather them or list them in order of priority

3. Create a digital or paper scrapbook of documents, press releases, and major achievements

4. For each item, decide if the motivation to achieve the documented milestone was an inner or outer motivation—or perhaps a combination

5. Select only those documented achievements that reflect an inner motivation

6. Focus on one incident during your journey toward achieving a documented milestone

7. Frame it into a narrative arc

8. Link it to the qualities of self that most define you

Events that lead to defining stories will continue to occur throughout your life. Practice keeping track of them in a journal, a scrapbook, or a digital album of photos and comments.

Storytellers Share Secrets: Defining Story

Having a series of defining stories is a valuable social and professional asset: they serve to introduce you to others in a memorable way in any setting. Whether you're in a job interview, meeting an online date, in dinner conversation, or at a party, a defining story is your sure way to make a lasting impression. Rather than recite a list of facts about yourself, you can simply provide a context for a story. Each one of these contributors are experts in their work, whether as storyteller or memoirist. They've spent decades learning how to shape and deliver a story. In fact, you might say that stories define them.

Creating

Linda Joy Myers, author of the award-winning memoir *Song of the Plains*, grew up in Enid, Oklahoma, where she experienced the power and beauty of the landscape and the people who marked her soul for life. She is the president and founder of the National Association of Memoir Writers. Linda Joy is the author of *The Power of Memoir* and *Journey of Memoir*, and coauthored *Breaking Ground on your Memoir* and *The Magic of Memoir*. She is a coach to beginning memoir writers and a host to memoir experts in frequent webinars and conferences. She is fully aware of how writers yearn to express the stories that need to be told.

The Urgency of Story

Linda Joy Myers

A story to be shared is one that will not leave you alone. It rests on your heart and pushes for you to share it, and, sometimes, just the right moment comes, or the right person, when you need to tell the story. Other times, the story presses against you at the wrong moment, so you adapt your strategy—you find how to tell it so it fits the moment. The story is looking for someone to hold the other end of a thread. Then there is a tuning in, like how you listen to the vibration of a musical instrument. You play the music of that story and adapt it to the person, situation, and your own need to tell it as it rests unformed on your lips. With each person with whom I share a story, I pull a different thread. Each time I tell it, I'm living the story, but my emotions afterward may be different, from exalted to sad or contemplative as the memories spin forth. The dreams in my defining story are alive as I tell it, and the other person in my story is always alive in my heart.

Linda Joy has decades of experience in working with memoir writers and in writing her own. She understands the subtle interaction between teller and listener, how each participates in making meaning of a story. No story is more profound than a defining story that works through the superficial layers of one's psyche to find a truth within one's self. How others react to our deepest stories is important, so we are cautioned to adapt them to our specific audiences. Linda Joy asks us to be aware of how we share our most precious stories: to know each person and situation and measure how listeners will react, along with developing awareness of our own need to tell. Linda Joy's first art as a young girl was music, playing the cello. Her sense of story is similar to that of a musical vibration, and she understands how to tune in to the listener—the audience. Live storytellers do so, and they participate in a creative interplay of story and imagination.

Crafting

A Kiss Goodbye, and Hello

Linda Joy Myers

I found myself in the middle of a story that spanned the arc of my life—it began when I was eleven back home in Oklahoma and ended when I was seventy-four. The new story changed the framework of how I remembered the past. It was as if two days together with my friend Keith after many years changed my history. Keith was my first love when I was eleven, and it became a mutual love when I was seventeen. He was kind; he saw me behind the glasses and the weird grandmother, and he knew me as no one had. I had seen him off and on in the fifty-six years since our prom, when we danced to "Moon River," and I'd called him on his birthday for years. But after the prom, our separation was forced by his family and mine, and we never talked about it…until the spring of my seventy-fourth year. For forty years, I dreamed about finding him: we were in love and reunited and happy. But in the last dream, he was dying. I called him and, yes, he was in hospice care. I flew back home to his side, and we got to talk over all the unsaid things. We time-traveled back to moments we'd shared, to music, Bach, and Beethoven, and the Hallelujah Chorus, golden wheat fields, and stars over the Great Plains sky.

We both came to understand what the dreams meant—that we were connected beyond time or space. What a blessing after so many years: what was not spoken or shared finally was. He asked if he could kiss me goodbye when I was leaving. Close, face to face, I saw in those brown eyes all the years of our lives we had shared, the essence of soul that lingered always on the strands of the music we loved, side by side in the cello section.

You are with the angels, my friend, and in my heart always. I'm more whole because I knew you. May you journey toward the heart of the universe and be with those you love.

In this defining story, Linda Joy shares a lifelong thread, a narrative that spanned her life from her childhood to elder years. It is a love story of many dimensions, one that transcends time and space, waking and sleeping. Because Linda Joy pays attention to the key stories in her life, she was able to observe her life narrative shift when she visited her first love on his deathbed. He had known her, her truest self, and had come to understand her through symphony music. The essence of joy they both shared playing as youths in the cello section of the orchestra was their bliss. In the story, Linda Joy says, "I'm more whole because I knew you," and gives us a kernel of deepest truth: we often see ourselves in the eyes of those who love us most

Creating

Bea Bowles is a storyteller, writer, and recording artist of wonder tales that connect children to nature's deep and lasting wisdom. She performs nationally and internationally in schools, botanical gardens, art and garden centers, and at conferences. Bea's audiobooks and CDs feature original music by composer Sara Buchanan MacLean. Always inspired by Spider Grandmother, the fairy godmother of storytelling, Bea weaves webs of stories from different cultures around a shared theme in performances and audio storybooks, as well as in her two storybooks, *Spider Secrets* and *Grandmother Spider's Web of Wonders*. How Bea became inspired to begin her work is her defining story.

Crafting

Grandmother Spider

Bea Bowles

On the first night of my first storytelling conference in Santa Fe, New Mexico, I stood outside under the stars, wondering what my role as a storyteller might be. A whisper came from the dark: "Teach children to wonder." Startled, I hurried inside.

Onstage, Jose Rey Toledo, a tall Hopi elder with long white braids, told a story of Spider Grandmother and Grandfather Sun, who sang and danced up all of creation: on three long, dangerous journeys led by Spider Grandmother, insects appeared, then animals, and finally people. Because people could learn, Spider Grandmother taught them to sing, dance, weave, grow crops, and give thanks for life on earth. But in time, evil leaders began to chant, "Fight, Hate, Hoard, Gamble." The people who listened ruined their world. Only a faithful few found their up way to this, the fourth world.

A tiny, caring spider and the mighty sun as grandparents of creation? That story still keeps me wondering. When Jose Rey gave me permission to tell the story, he added, "Grandmother Spider whispers wisdom to guide children today, too, so remind them to listen."

In time, I learned other creation stories from around the world, and here in Northern California, Malcolm Margolin introduced me to the great Achomawi writer, Darryl "Babe" Wilson. So spider stories became the repertoire for my first storytelling events and my first storybook, *Spider Secrets*.

I proposed to New Dimensions Radio that I record the Hopi story and other creation stories as a children's production. They agreed and assigned Joseph Campbell as my mentor, so following my bliss proved a good idea. Though I tell many kinds of wonder tales now, I give thanks to spiders, to the sun, and to stories every morning.

Bea Bowles was deeply connected to both nature and stories as she sought her role as a storyteller in this personal tale. It's not surprising that she heard a whisper in the night air, an intuitive voice. Often, tuning in to an inner voice is a pathway to the inner self. Whispers, stories that surface, images that won't leave us, and dreams that come to us all contain messages that can define us. When Bea heard the Hopi story of Grandmother Spider, she was both mesmerized and amazed—she connected to the mythic character in ways that reflected her own nature. In a subtle and artistic way, Bea and the spider/mother archetype merged with Bea the storyteller to create an authentic brand. That she learned more about the deeper layers of folklore with Joseph Campbell as her mentor speaks to her commitment to the art. But there is no doubt that Grandmother Spider is Bea's power story, her totem, and her defining message.

Signature Story

First made popular by Toastmasters International, **signature stories continue to evolve in mainstream culture**. Sometimes called the elevator speech, a signature story is a short, well-crafted pitch that introduces you professionally or personally. It is certainly an essential tool for self-marketing. Even though it is a short presentation and is often delivered one-on-one, it is still prepared with as much care as you would a major keynote address. Its basic story elements can be structured as a simple, outlined script so that the content is adaptable for a variety of situations and is conversational in tone.

The first sentence—the 'hook'—is the most important, and it might very well contain the entire signature speech in a condensed version. Introduce yourself as a solution to a problem, one that is faced by your colleagues in your target profession or market. Job titles and resume-type information are not appropriate in a signature story. Your clients are only interested in how you can help them in their personal or professional life. The first sentence gets to the point in plain terms, the point being to engage your listeners and tweak their interest. For example, a life coach might introduce herself by saying, "I coach people in how to open closed doors."

The central element is a personal anecdote that describes your motivation—your *aha* moment in the field—or an example that demonstrates your expertise. **The story is the heart of the pitch**, and it is also how you create a bond with your listeners. The more compelling the story, the more unforgettable it will be. No matter how short, it is still a complete narrative with specific details, vivid language, dialogue, and a clear story structure. The entire signature story, including hook and narrative, takes no more than two to three minutes to tell. Keep a few signature stories on hand for different audiences, like a neighborhood party or a networking event.

A professional signature story is simple to define and easy enough to formulate. But how do you arrive at the content? One way is to recall your most successful experience in a given profession or how you overcame a challenge in your work. What was your breakthrough moment? Is it motivating enough to share? Signature stories highlight the best of your professional experience: they help define not only what makes you successful, but also what gives you joy and your career meaning.

According to David Asker, author of *Creating Signature Stories*, professional signature stories have great value for your personal life as well.

Finding such stories can help you discover a purpose, set priorities, gain confidence, develop new directions, enhance relationships, engage in a program to gain strengths, and more.

Creating

The professional signature story is targeted to your career and its goals. While a defining story is open-ended and is a deep sharing of self, a signature story is focused on breakthrough moments in your vocation or avocation—with powerful insights you are motivated to share, and even to market and sell.

Though short, a signature story should be a complete narrative, with its outcome clearly stated. For a signature story to hold your listeners' attention and have a lasting impact, it needs to have the entire complement of an unforgettable tale:

- Setting: Where did it take place—in what professional setting?

- Conflict: What was the essential problem, crisis, disagreement, or challenge?

- Action: What are the scenes in the story—the rising action?

- Who are the real-life characters?

- What is the dialogue?

- Finally, what is the breakthrough moment or resolution?

- Based on this experience, what is your hook? Is it perhaps the introduction to the story?

The following signature story is one I've told countless times: at the beginning of storytelling training sessions, in talks on the power of storytelling, and as a pitch to foundation executives and to influential publishers. This story has been an unqualified success in opening doors. More importantly, it gave me the opportunity to share what I'd learned with many thousands of educators and writers in my field.

San Francisco Junior High School 1967

I stood behind the lectern, my place of refuge, and looked out at my ninth-grade students crammed into every desk in the bleak, overcrowded, urban classroom. It was the dreaded period right after lunch on a hot spring day, and I was to teach them English. I'd already realized in this, my first year of teaching, that most of my students could not read or write at grade level, if at all.

My immediate solution had been, "Well, if they can't read the literature, I'll read it for them." Over the months, I'd read aloud from the assigned, grade-level texts: *Arabian Nights*, *Old Yeller*, *Great Expectations*, and Greek mythology. Gripping the rickety, plywood lectern, I'd held sway over my classes with dramatic interpretations.

On that day, I'd prepared to read aloud a Greek myth. Irked at the tired textbook prose, I realized I couldn't bear to read another myth from that boring book. I stepped away from the lectern. I stood in front of the class. The class looked at me with some apprehension—I don't think they'd seen my legs before. I began to tell them, in my own words, the tale that was next in the book, the story of Daphne and Apollo.

I will never forget the change in the room: suddenly there was nothing else in it except my words and the students' eyes, watching. They were looking at me with the greatest attention I'd ever received, but at the same time I knew they were not seeing me at all. They were seeing beyond me, into the myth. In fact, both the students and I were watching the adventure of Daphne and Apollo as it took place.

The classroom itself was transformed. It seemed to become the far-off Greek forest of long ago, with tangled green foliage and splashing streams. For the length of the story, we were there. It was electrifying! And I was no longer bored. No, I was never to forget that day's experience.

Crafting

When I tell this story, I start at the brink of the action on that fateful day and depict the problem: teaching English literature to ninth-grade students who could barely read or write. Even though I've told this signature story countless times, its key details trigger my memory once again. So, it's important to note the time of day and season, the overcrowded classroom, the feel of the plywood lectern—even the titles of the books I'd read aloud that year. Most important is the name of the exact myth, the story of Daphne and Apollo. Each essential story element places me at that precise time and place so that I can stand in the middle of the experience and observe it unfold.

The story itself is elastic; it can take thirty seconds or up to three minutes to tell, depending on the situation. But there are specific details to bear in mind and retain—conflict, rising action, resolution. One of them is the hook: **I became a storyteller to teach inner-city students literature.** This summary statement can be told at the beginning or the end of the story. Either way, it's a tribute to the power of storytelling to connect in difficult circumstances.

The myth of Daphne and Apollo is the story within the story, similar to the dragon tale in my defining story. It is vital to recall the details of the myth in order to visualize the effect of telling it to the ninth-grade students. Each time, I refresh my memory of the setting and the myth's conflict set in motion by Eros and his arrows of gold and lead, the rescue brought about by Daphne's father, Peneus. I review the main action, the chase scene: Apollo chasing the frightened wood nymph through the dense forest and Daphne's sudden metamorphosis into a laurel tree; Apollo then claims the laurel branch as his crowning, heroic honor, in memory of his beloved Daphne.

Researching the myth and its basic elements is part of my preparation, and doing so facilitates my memories of that day—they highlight the immediate appeal of that particular myth.

Layers of Meaning

As you deepen your understanding of your signature story, you become aware of elements and layers within it that are not readily apparent. Knowing them provides a depth to your telling and prepares you to answer questions about the incident. In the example story, "San Francisco Junior HS 1967," there were unique layers—often communicated between the lines:

- Desperation of a first-year, white English teacher in a black community

- Long, hot summers of race riots, 1965, 1966, and 1967, that included the school's community

- Counterculture in San Francisco, simultaneous to the Civil Rights Movement of 1965, 1966, and 1967

- Lack of school funding in the underserved black community

- High attrition rate among teachers and administrators

- Rigidly assigned textbooks by grade level, citywide

- Lack of teaching materials, limited to textbooks, blackboard, chalk

- Power of myth and storytelling to transcend time, place, and culture

- Strategy for class management as well as teaching—created a personal bond

There is no need to belabor the dire situation in that 1967 classroom in the Bayview District of San Francisco within the story itself. It is sufficient to tell a few hard facts to convey the bleak learning environment. However, if in telling the story to a particular group, you are prepared to embellish, to answer questions, and to talk about the history of the era and your success with that myth, you will further engage listeners. Obviously, this 1967 classroom was low-tech, reduced to its most basic needs. After decades of high-speed, wide-band progress, I often wonder if the high-tech classrooms are more effective.

Telling

Your signature story is uniquely yours and is often a synthesis of years of experience and trial and error. When you review the insights you brought to a problem, you'll uncover how these reflect your essential character. This in turn will affect how you tell the story and its tone, emotional impact, and purpose.

A signature story depends on an economy of words to be effective. It is, after all, your pitch, an abbreviated, memorable way to sell your expertise.

Outline the basic structure of the story with its problems and their solution within a clear narrative arc. Once structured, this story can be adapted to any circumstance without the need to memorize.

For "San Francisco Junior High School 1967," the outline is simple:

1. Setting: an overcrowded, inner-city classroom

2. Characters: first-year white teacher, thirty-five students, black, Latinx, poor white

3. First scene: after lunch, reading aloud to functionally illiterate class, boring

4. Second scene: step away from lectern and book, rising action

5. Third scene: tell a Greek myth in my own words, directly to class

6. Resolution: active and creative listening, rapt attention, basis for discussion and teaching

7. Conclusion: unforgettable, share the insight

Keep your signature story outline with your resume, pitch, or talking points for public speaking. At conferences or professional meetings, have it handy to refresh your memory.

Refer to Chapter Four for other ways to capture the signature story through graphic prompts, along with tips for its effective delivery.

The "Seven Steps to Storytelling" were original to the Word Weaving Storytelling Project and featured throughout its highly successful trainings for educators. These demystify the art of storytelling into easy-to-learn steps.

Exercises & Prompts: Signature Story

Prompts: Professional Signature Story

Answer these prompts to find or create a **professional** signature story. If you have a few career tracks, fix one profession in your mind. Each career path will have its own signature story—its breakthrough narrative.

1. Look back on your years in a given profession

2. What was your motivation?

3. What are your strengths and weaknesses in the field?

4. Who are your role models or mentors?

5. What are your greatest career successes?

6. Describe your highest achievement

7. What problem did you solve that you'd like to share?

8. What was your *aha* moment?

9. Was it a sudden revelation, or did it occur over time?

Prompts: Personal Signature Story

Answer these prompts to find or create a **personal** signature story, one that reflects the best of you:

1.   Look back on your last year or decade

2.   What experiences gave you the most happiness or meaning?

3.   What people do you remember the most?

4.   What interactions represented the best in your relationships?

5.   What events demonstrated your truest instincts?

6.   What situations gave you joy, relief, pride, or admiration?

7.   In what personal setting(s) do you feel most content?

8.   When did you feel closest to a personal truth?

9.   How have you shared your personal story, or how could you share it?

Storytellers Share Secrets: Signature Story

These multitalented professionals are consultants, public speakers, coaches, and published authors. Their work in the literary field has been award-winning and varied in both genre and media: they have crossed over to corporate work and have mastered the skill of promoting their services.

Creating

Betsy Graziani Fasbinder is an author, psychotherapist, podcaster, public speaking teacher, and coach. Whether in our intimate conversations, our written stories, or our professional lives, it is Betsy's belief that our stories make the deepest connections. She is the host of the Morning Glory Project: Stories of Determination, as well as author of a novel, *Fire & Water*, a memoir, *Filling Her Shoes*, and an instructive nonfiction book, *From Page to Stage: Inspiration, Tools, and Public Speaking Tips for Writers*.

Spellbinders

Betsy Graziani Fasbinder

The irony of my signature story, which depicts my intense fear of public speaking, is that I tell it today to participants in my public speaking classes. Though I'm a writer and author, as my "day job," I've been a teacher and coach of public speaking for more than twenty years, working in America's largest companies with participants at all levels of organizations from new hires to CEOs, across industries. I've coached executives and sales teams, politicians, entrepreneurs, writers, artists, TED Talkers, and gun violence survivors drafted into activism by tragedy.

I always coach my clients to think of themselves as storytellers, not as data disseminators. It's stories, not facts, that are memorable and engage audiences, inspiring them to a shift in attitude or to take action. Stories should be specific, relevant, and memorable for maximum impact. I call these mini-stories as part of a talk "Spellbinders." Stories that captivate the imaginations or emotions of listeners cast a "spell" during which inspiration and influence can be achieved.

Fear, or at least nervousness, about public speaking is not universal, but it's close. Most people think that dynamic public speaking is a gift that some people have and others just don't. I'm proof that this is not true. By learning a set of simple skills (that I now teach), I was able to manage my fears and to use my voice for the causes that matter most to me.

I use the "Spellbinder," or my signature story, about Mr. Ellis to illustrate that no matter how fearful or unskilled we might be, anyone can become a dynamic speaker. By demonstrating public speaking skills with confidence and sharing my beginnings, I am the proof of the point to my students. Of course, some people come to public speaking more naturally than others (though I was *not* a natural)—the same is true for any art. It's by learning and practicing a handful of simple skills—including the use of spellbinding stories—that we can overcome our fears and begin to see the possibilities for our own powers as captivating storytellers.

It's clear that Betsy Graziani Fasbinder has a strong voice in her written work; her public speaking voice is equally engaging. But she is clever enough to know that sharing the truth of her journey as a public speech coach is a not only a training tool, but a marketing tool. Most people, no matter the field, fear speaking in public. Because Betsy had the same fear and overcame it, having solved the dreaded problem, her experience is a convincing example to promote her speaking skills: What she learned, anyone can.

Crafting

The Spellbinding Power of Story

Betsy Graziani Fasbinder

I was impossibly shy in my youth. Aside from graduating and getting scholarships to college, my primary goal in high school was to be invisible; I largely met my goal. As a sophomore, I had an English teacher and mentor who fostered my love of stories and encouraged my talents in writing. My future life as an author was born of his mentoring. As a junior, I also had Mr. Ellis for the required class that I most dreaded: speech.

For an invisible girl, thoughts of delivering five three-minute speeches to my classmates created an avalanche of anxiety. The week before the first speech, after I'd prepared the content, I approached Mr. Ellis in a weepy puddle. I'd suffered insomnia for days: bellyaches, headaches, and fear hounded me to distraction. "I just can't do it," I told him, sobbing.

Mr. Ellis patted my shoulder in a fatherly way. "Okay," he said. "I have a deal for you." He offered me an alternative. If I'd write a twenty-page term paper about a great speech in history, complete with footnotes and at least three cited references (this was long before computers and the internet), he'd accept that in lieu of a speech. I'm sure he set the bar at that ridiculous level thinking that I'd surely reject his offer.

"Absolutely!" I said, and we shook hands on the deal. Not only did I accept his deal, I begged him to allow it for all five speeches, and my softy teacher with a kind affection for his shy student agreed.

> Do the math. At sixteen, I wrote one hundred pages on five research topics to avoid fifteen minutes of speaking in front of my class.

This is such a perfect signature story because it has all the elements of a compelling narrative: setting, conflict, characters, and dialogue. It draws us in, simply to hear a story, so that the magic, the spellbinding, can take over. Betsy is conscious of the power of storytelling and does not skim to summarize; she slows down the main action to accommodate a natural telling. She lets us feel her symptoms and her anxiety and makes us feel as if we participate in the interaction with her teacher who patted her shoulder so kindly. All the features of excellent storytelling technique are present. At the same time, she is using her past fear as a way to qualify her as the best coach—for those who fear public speaking. Her story of Mr. Ellis illustrates that no matter how fearful or unskilled we might be, anyone can become a dynamic speaker.

Creating

Joan Gelfand is the author of *You Can Be a Winning Writer*, a writing coach, and a speaker to writing groups. She has written three acclaimed volumes of poetry, an award-winning chapbook of short fiction, and *Fear to Shred*, a novel set in a Silicon Valley startup. The recipient of numerous writing awards, commendations, nominations, and honors, Joan is a member of the National Book Critics Circle and Bay Area Travel Writers and a past president of the Women's National

Book Association. She is a juror for the Northern California Book Awards.

Author's Backstory

Joan Gelfand

I cannot stress enough how important it is to share our "backstories." How did we get on that podium, stage, or TV or become the subject of that radio or magazine interview? So many times, aspiring writers idealize the journey of a successful writer, performer, or artist. It's not their fault; they see someone on stage, communicating and inspiring others, and just think *magic happens*. But so often, and most certainly in my case, there were years of work that went into that performance, talk, or lecture. When I meet people and say I have six published books, their reaction is sometimes respect, but often they are intimidated. It took me six years after I began writing to identify as a writer and then decades to get serious about publishing. I had to build my stamina for rejection; I had to cultivate mettle, a professional detachment from my emotional response to rejection.

In my workshops and in coaching my clients, I share the vicissitudes of my journey: how long it took, how many rejections. I speak about a consistent program of submissions and how success builds on success. I share how my confidence was built on confidence. A first publication, and then another, started the ball rolling. But that first step can often lead to door upon door opening up and opportunities being presented.

Joan uses the frustration of her own career experience of becoming a traditionally published author to encourage and inform both her writing clients and her fellow writers. Her belief is not that she should add to the fantasy that many beginning writers continue to have: that their book will "catch on," that Oprah will call, or that an online listing on Amazon will create a bestseller. By sharing her honest and practical approach, Joan has been able to publish a book on the topic, one that includes her signature story, and develop a promotional program for writers.

Crafting

Novel Fever

Joan Gelfand

Early in my career, after some marked success as a poet, I got bitten by "novel fever." Post-college, I had had a fair number of poems published in literary journals. I had performed at prestigious venues like the Oakland Museum, Litquake, and the Beat Museum. I had even had the excellent fortune to have a poem turned into a song and recorded by a rock band. The song was aired on the local radio station and nationally. But I still didn't feel like a winning writer.

I didn't set out to write a novel. *I mean, really?* I had cut my teeth on Simone de Beauvoir, Virginia Woolf, Willa Cather, Kurt Vonnegut, Gunter Grass, and Wallace Stegner. I was satisfied being a poet known to my local community.

Writing a novel seemed like a terribly pretentious, misguided idea. No. I did not start out to write a novel. I started out with a story that, after two years and much encouragement from my writing instructor, grew into three hundred pages. I had written my first novel without planning to do so.

It was with that first novel that I began to understand that becoming a successful writer wasn't just about writing. It was several years after my first attempt to find a publisher for that first novel that I understood the business of writing.

I learned that the letter I got back from an agent asking me to revise my manuscript was a serious request, not a rejection. And I learned the hard way that without confidence, without commitment, and without community, I was never going to become a winning writer.

Joan's signature story, one she's used in her recent book, *You Can Be a Winning Writer*, is a powerful one. She learned over years of dreaming of authoring a novel that writing is a business. Now, she is not only publishing her first novel, but sharing the process with her clients and writers in her community. It is part of her legacy that Joan gives back, with the hope that others do not delay or defer their writing dreams. No doubt the business of traditional publishing is a daunting one and a hard one to crack. But Joan is clear that a combination of qualities, a holistic approach, can open the doors. She also sees there are many measures of writing success and that each author determines what success means: local, national, international. Joan may have backed into her dream and made it come true, but she doesn't think her clients have to do the same. Her signature story tells us that she now knows how to walk through the front door of a publishing house.

Personal Brand Story

A personal brand story derives from defining stories and signature stories by crystalizing self-definition and self-presentation in the marketplace into a brief, compelling narrative. This authentic, organic process reflects your motivation and success in a way that connects you personally to your customer and promotes a service or product. A personal brand story uses the art of storytelling to convey value in a core message by weaving both facts and narrative together in a captivating way.

But why should we choose storytelling over a data-driven slideshow or a bulleted list? Why have stories become the go-to way of sharing, explaining, and selling? Because stories, by their very nature, entertain, inspire, and motivate. They can simplify a complicated message with an unforgettable narrative and reach across consumer differences. Despite our language, religion, political preferences, or ethnicity, stories connect us—if they are genuine. Storytelling is a universal language that everyone understands, a language as old as time, one that touches our common humanity.

When we use a mastery of storytelling to create a personal brand story, we are part of a long and evocative tradition—one with the potential to attract new customers and create loyal ones. The art of storytelling engages its audience more completely than facts do. It involves more of the human brain, both left and right hemispheres, as well as emotions, passions, and memories. Stories create pictures with words through specific, sensory descriptions; they create drama through a rise and fall of action; and finally, they provide a resolution that can include a call to action.

Recently, storytelling has become a vital component of the most successful marketing campaigns. Tips on how to create brand content in storytelling formats fill the internet. It is the one marketing tool that seems to rise above the noise and sets apart exciting brands from ordinary businesses or services. As our attention spans burn out and the amount of internet content soars, it has become more important than ever to know how to tell a good story. A brand story can become a powerful vicarious experience for its target audience, one they internalize as if they lived it. **Listeners become the hero of every story they hear**. As such, a story has a lasting imprint—if it is well told.

Creating

What is and what isn't a brand story? It's much easier to categorize what is *not* a brand story: sales goals, an advertisement, a long article, bullet points, a PowerPoint presentation, or a sales pitch that is "about" your brand.

For a brand story to engage, it needs to have all the components of a good story, with useful information woven into its fabric:

- Audience: Identify the target audience. Who wants to hear your story? Who will benefit?

- Core message: What is the point? Define it in six to ten words.

- Characters: Who are the characters? It could be you!

- Conflict: What was the essential problem, crisis, or challenge?

- Action: What are the scenes in the story that make up the rising action?

- Finally, what is the resolution?

- Based on this experience, what is the call to action? What do you want your audience to do?

Using my own process as an example, I reviewed my defining and signature stories and selected particular personal details and facts to condense my narrative into a brief form, ending with a core message and a call to action. This brand story retains the authenticity of longer stories, but is targeted to a local network of educators, storytellers, and writers.

Storyteller

Kate Farrell was a storyteller at an early age. By age ten, she'd tacked signs on telephone poles in her neighborhood announcing her fairy-tale play. As a first-year teacher, she stumbled onto storytelling as the best way to teach literature to inner-city kids. By 1970, she'd honed the skill as a new librarian, and in 1980, she funded and trained teachers in a California statewide storytelling project—then, she published educational materials on the art with big name publishers like Scholastic and Highlights for Children. In the ever-evolving world of storytelling, by 2005, Farrell understood that personal narrative was the new folklore—so, she wrote and edited memoir anthologies. Farrell's work is a bridge in storytelling: from traditional folklore to authentic, personal tales. Contact her for trainings and talks on this powerful art.

Crafting

In crafting my personal brand story, I reviewed my own incidents of self-discovery in the other two stories in this chapter, the defining story and the signature story. It was a personal breakthrough to recognize similar threads woven throughout these tales, from childhood to the present. Authenticity establishes credibility in this case: I was true to my bliss without encouragement and sometimes in spite of active resistance. The success of my work in storytelling, from the aha moment in the classroom to training thousands of teachers and publishing storytelling materials showed, an entrepreneurial spirit.

However, it was my willingness to keep up with the changes in contemporary storytelling, in what had been an unbroken, oral tradition for centuries, that depicted the true strength of my brand: the bridge between old and new traditions. And so, that is the core message: **Farrell's work is a bridge in storytelling: from traditional folklore to authentic, personal tales.**

There are some sensory images, such as "tacking signs on telephone poles" and "stumbled." But for the most part, my brand story is a sequential narrative with clear markers in the dates cited along the way. It was a journey of many decades. The implicit conflict was how to promote and adapt the ancient tradition of storytelling to modern times. The call to action is simple, since mine is a personal consulting service.

Like a resume, the brand story is told in the **third person.** In order to compress the information and present it as a brand, it seems the best device is to distance yourself from your own story. Tell it as the narrator so that the listener can more easily identify with it.

The process outlined in this chapter can lead to an authentic personal brand story—use the exercises and prompts for the defining story and signature story to create a condensed version.

Layers of Meaning

By definition, the personal brand story has many layers of meaning: it is compressed from key experiences over time to support a core message. It is brief and to the point, while at the same time retaining the basic elements of a true story, blending fact with information. Knowing those facts and the details of the brand story provides a depth to your telling, and it prepares you to either answer questions about the incident or to enlarge on the synopsis in another setting. In my sample brand story, "Storyteller," there are unique layers—some personal, and some that coincide with the rise and fall of the storytelling tradition and its ancient folklore:

- Unsupervised walks to the Roosevelt Library in San Antonio, blocks from my house, as a child

- Independently discovering the *Andrew Lang Fairy Books*, in their array of colors on a low shelf

- The allure of fairy tales, constant return to the library to borrow books in the twenty-seven-book series

- Demonstrated power of storytelling Greek myths, inner-city school: refer to signature story

- Independent funding for storytelling with California Department of Education: refer to defining story

- Training of trainers in California and Nevada public schools, thirteen-year project and partnership

- Unprecedented contracts with high profile publishers for storytelling educational materials

- Decline of folktales and the art of live storytelling; the conflicts of cultural appropriation

- Rise of personal narrative, memoir, and journaling as a new tradition

- Interest in storytelling in mainstream culture: Moth, TED, marketing tools, branding

- Study of personal narrative and memoir writing, technique and purpose, editing anthologies

- Ability to see elements of folklore in personal narratives

So much is packed into a personal brand story: there are stories within stories for each line. Each statement is a trigger and could be used as such in live presentations. The personal brand story is a powerful tool. It not only can clarify your career journey, but your own motivation and core message. It is a useful practice for both you as the creator and for those listeners who respond to your call to action.

Telling

As you consider the potential impact of your brand story, continue to refine it for a variety of presentations and adapt it to each one.

Your personal brand story is already extremely condensed. As a memory aid, you could reduce it further to a set of bullet points. By so doing, you'll avoid remembering it as a set piece when telling it live.

Outline the story, stripping details down to keywords indicating its narrative arc.

For my "Storyteller" brand story, the outline is simple:

1. Characters: Neighbors, students, teachers, funders, publishers, writers

2. First scene: Childhood neighborhood, early interest in fairy tales

3. Second scene: Teacher, storytelling as a teaching strategy, professional trainings, statewide

4. Third scene: Author with high profile, national publishers

5. Fourth scene: Storytelling tradition evolving, personal narrative

6. Conclusion: Core message, call to action

The personal brand story might not be told live and in person. It certainly could be, as a short signature story. But it also might appear as text on a website, postcard, or promotional printed material.

Chapter Four offers other methods for crafting and remembering your personal brand story, including graphic prompts such as a story map, mind map, or storyboard. You'll also discover some key tips for effectively delivering even a short story.

The "Seven Steps to Storytelling" were original to the Word Weaving Storytelling Project and featured throughout its highly successful, professional trainings for educators. These demystify the art of storytelling into easy-to-learn steps.

Exercises & Prompts: Personal Brand Story

Exercises: Personal Brand Story

1. Reflect on decisive story choices in creating and crafting your defining story

2. Select key story elements from your signature story

3. If you have not created a signature story, use those story prompts now

4. Construct a series of events that led you to your career mission today, using both story types as guides or triggers

5. Consider an event from your earliest years, one that demonstrated your passion or mission

6. Develop a narrative that shows your continued motivation over time

7. Write a condensed timeline as a narrative arc

8. Show how these events still drive your mission

9. Introduce some sensory details along with specific facts

10. Create empathy for your character by writing about yourself in the third person

11. Make it possible for listeners to enter into your story as the main character—to identify and bond

12. Write your core message and call to action

This process assumes that every event is true, authentic, and one you directly experienced. In this personal brand story, each word or incident is meaningful—no cheating on the facts. Continue working, editing, crystalizing until your brand story is no more than ten sentences.

Storytellers Share Secrets: Personal Brand Story

Having a personal brand story is a boon for published authors, since they are constantly introducing themselves at book readings, on a book tour, or before a talk. They need to have a quick introductory story to immediately appeal to their readers—their fan base. These stories show their commitment to their writing career in reaching their readers, illustrated by the number of rejections they received from publishers and by their passion to follow their writing career. The personal brand story is excellent for the back flap of a book's dust jacket or on a website's home page. It can also be used as an engaging way for the author to be introduced.

Creating

Marissa Moss, award-winning children's author and illustrator, has produced many popular picture books, as well as a series of readers featuring a young writer named Amelia, beginning with *Amelia's Notebook*. Marissa has written historical journals, also in diary format. Marissa's keen interest in history and her passion to share notable events of history with children has prompted her to continue to produce award-winning picture books, such as *Barb Wired Baseball* and *The Eye That Never Sleeps: How Detective Pinkerton Saved President Lincoln*.

Crafting

Children's Author & Illustrator

Marissa Moss has told stories and drawn pictures for as long as she can remember—even on the furniture. She took her first art class when she was five, submitted her first picture book to publishers when she was nine (it was rejected, of course), illustrated her first published book in

> high school, and drew her way all through college. Making picture books was all she ever wanted to do, even after receiving a whole shoeboxfull of rejection letters from editors. While buying school supplies for her son, she saw a black-and-white splotched composition book that reminded her of one she had when she was nine—that's how *Amelia's Notebook* came to be. Today, Marissa has published over seventy books and is working on new formats. Keep your eye on her website to see what she's drawing and writing next!

Marissa's readers are children, grade school through middle school students. Her books are typically a charming mix of text and line drawings executed in an ingenuous style. Like her published works, her personal brand story has a direct line to her young readers: she is like them, someone who drew on the walls or the furniture as a preschooler. Her readers can identify with Marissa as someone who was once willful and creative, but who never lost touch with her childhood dreams. Marissa's story is effective because she uses specific details, such as the "shoeboxfull" and the "black-and-white splotched composition book." She compresses the timeline of her career into a clear narrative arc with its impressive result of seventy published books. When the readers are asked to keep an eye on her website, they are motivated to see what might come next due to the underlying enthusiasm throughout Marissa's story.

Creating

S.G. Browne is a writer of dark comedy and social satire with a supernatural or fantastic edge. He writes about zombies

fighting for their civil rights, private detectives born with the
ability to steal luck, and professional guinea pigs who test
pharmaceutical drugs and develop unusual superpowers.
His published works include the novels *Breathers*, *Fated*,
Lucky Bastard, *Big Egos*, and *Less Than Hero*, as well as
the short story collection *Shooting Monkeys in a Barrel* and
the heartwarming holiday novella, *I Saw Zombies Eating
Santa Claus*.

Crafting

Fantasy Fiction

S.G. Browne grew up with a love of math and science
he expected would play a role in his career path. But,
during college, he discovered his creative side, writing
and directing his fraternity's entry into an annual stage
competition called "Band Frolic." After college, he worked in
Hollywood at a postproduction studio hoping to break into
the movies writing screenplays, before moving to Santa
Cruz to write his first novel. Four novels, dozens of short
stories, and hundreds of rejection letters later, he published
Breathers, the first of his five socially satirical novels. Check
out his website for updated news and stories.

S. G.'s personal brand story is authentic and fascinating,
with all the twists and turns of a novel itself. Nevertheless,
he remains true to his creative vision in it—his youthful
passion to write and engage an audience, whether in a staged
performance, a movie, or a novel. That he was first enamored of

math and science makes us wonder if and how he incorporated those interests into his fictional work. His use of specific detail works in this short narrative, such as his "fraternity's entry" and the name of their play, "Band Frolic." We are able to participate in his hopes and dreams as he pursues Hollywood, then a publisher. Readers applaud when their author shows commitment in his quest for publication, and they experience his success vicariously. S. G.'s story does all that and more: He intrigues us with a promise of stories and books to come.

Such Stuff

To be a person is to have a story to tell.

—Isak Dinesen

In this chapter, we've covered exciting new territory for the art of storytelling, that of public self-presentation for personal and professional use. Knowing your own motivations, essential character, and innate skills can be leverage in the marketplace—when told as a story.

This chapter models these three story types:

- **Defining stories are at the heart of self-discovery** and have the power to express one's unique identity to others.

- **A Signature Story** is a short, well-crafted pitch that introduces you professionally or personally, an essential tool for self-marketing a service or product.

- **The Personal Brand Story** crystallizes self-presentation in the marketplace into a very brief, compelling narrative that reflects your motivation and success, personally connecting you to your customer to promote a service or product.

Even the shortest, most compressed story must contain the essential elements of a personal narrative to be effective and memorable:

- Setting
- Characters
- Conflict, tension

- Narrative arc of rising action, increasing tension
- Sensory images within the action
- Dialogue within the action, if possible
- Resolution of conflict

Six contributors shared examples of the three story types that demonstrate how stories can be effective promotional tools when used in a variety of formats: print, online, and in person. Through the contributors' tips and story excerpts, we've revealed the breakthrough moments in their lives and careers. Further, we've modeled how doing research and finding layers of meaning within each curated tale adds to their depth and their ability to connect to your audience or customer.

It's true that you can come to know yourself through the art of storytelling, if you are paying attention. If you are the unseen eyewitness to your actions, you will recognize yourself through your choices, trials, challenges, joys, and outcomes. With a cultivated honesty, you can begin to appreciate and accept the person you are by recording your everyday stories. This practice is beneficial to you, the storyteller, in many ways. By coming to know yourself through personal stories, you are more aware of the consequences of your actions. Your passions rise to the surface, your wisdom speaks, the voice of your experience tells your truths.

The inner eye, the one that observes oneself, is sometimes difficult to train, but it is worth the effort. In the golden mirror of that reflective practice, the magic to influence others is found. Telling a good story based on your experiences is like giving a mini-documentary of what you have seen so others can see it, too. When you share your knowledge through a targeted story, you access the power of story—the oldest tool known to influence and persuade throughout human history.

Chapter Three

Family Stories: How We Lived and Loved

This packrat has learned that what the next generation
will value most is not what we owned,
but the evidence of who we were and the tales of how we loved.
In the end, it's the family stories that are worth the storage.

—Ellen Goodman, journalist

Introduction

Our family, our tribe. However or whomever we identify as *family* is our tribe. We are bound together through our common experiences, our heritage, by blood or by intimate connection. And just as the tribal stories of old were shared through the oral tradition, so are ours. We learn our family stories in the memories we tell when we are gathered together for holidays, feasts, and celebrations—and, above all, in those stories that are repeated over time. These are the tales that communicate our values, character, identity, and how we make meaning of the world around us. In a sense, our combined body of stories creates family.

How do we preserve our quintessential family stories? As Ellen Goodman states, family stories have the greatest value to the next generation and "are worth the storage."

In the past, it was the traditional storyteller who connected the past to the future, who passed on tribal history, values, taboos, and the meaning of experiences and dreams. Often this was an elder, perhaps a crone who'd learned the tales from her aged mentor as a young apprentice. Without the benefit of print, the tribe's treasured tales, myths, and legends were committed to memory and survived centuries.

It could be that pictographs on stone and in caves were memory aids for the tribe and its storytellers. Drawings on tree bark, in sand, or with leaves displayed story motifs. Ritual dances, such as the Polynesian hula, enacted ancient stories through a complexity of gestures and rhythm. In songs and chants, poetry with a consistent beat and phrasing helped the storyteller to remember long narratives, even epics told over many days. Tattoos, face painting, and body painting brandished symbolic information about group origins and myths.

Contemporary society today provides ever-evolving options for digital storage: word processing programs, blogs, email, social media, chats, text, and instant messaging, along with visual display boards, video platforms and conferencing, and photo albums in the cloud. In spite of these many options, our family stories can remain ephemeral and may easily dissipate. Family legacy stories can lose their substance over time as electronic media takes center stage in our daily lives. The live human voice might seem old-fashioned, the storyteller outdated, our personal histories unimportant.

Often the memories we share with family members are fragmented and fluid, without a clear purpose in their telling. We might ignore significant family stories from the past or neglect to add more recent experiences. Over time, family tales can become random or superficial—their meaning lost. Yet our family stories, once shaped into memorable forms, can still be saved and passed down through the generations. Just as preliterate tribes shared a common sense of identity, history, and values in their stories, so we can discover exciting new ways to both preserve and create a family tradition of storytelling.

There is no real substitute for the live human exchange that is the hallmark of the oral tradition, but there are ways to document and record the raw material of family stories. By learning the techniques in this chapter and understanding how to create, frame, and tell family stories, you will ensure that important family stories become fully articulated and shaped into a story format, so they are ready to tell and retell in a variety of media.

Family stories matter. Family stories directly impact how we see ourselves because they give us an idea of where we come from and where we're going. Each family story is a pattern in a patchwork quilt of many colors and fabrics. Like the pieces in a multicolored, homemade quilt, our family stories are a combination of the cultures, histories, and traditions we've inherited. **And just like an embracing quilt, our stories bring us comfort: they give us a sense of belonging and create a core identity that can be a great source of empowerment.** Sharing family stories can give our children an emerging sense of self, both as individuals and as members of a family. Family members overall can enjoy higher self-esteem and greater resilience because they are able to draw from a deep, ancestral identity and contribute to it.

According to family narrative researcher Robyn Fivush, author of *Family Narratives and the Development of an Autobiographical Self*, there is value for both the listeners and the tellers in an ongoing, dynamic exchange:

> So, sharing family stories is certainly about passing down life lessons to the next generation. But it is also about hearing our own stories reflected through the eyes of others and learning something new about ourselves.

If we don't preserve our family legacy through its central narratives, we will lose it by default. Each generation will be defined by the mainstream media and given a superficial group identity: boomers, millennials, immigrants, etc. **In this chapter, we'll discuss how to create, frame, and tell**

family stories before they vanish. Using the techniques of storytelling, we'll salvage our cherished stories—our family folklore, secrets and shadows, and legacy tales.

Family Folklore

Family folklore is a ragbag collection of true stories and traditions gathered from the remembered experiences of generations past and present. It is transmitted through the art of storytelling, either in person or recorded. Storytelling is the main difference between family folklore and the study of genealogy or family history—those record data and information of the past. Family folklore is the age-old custom of passing down stories by word of mouth from one generation to the next. Since family folklore exists as part of the day-to-day life of a family, it is always changing and growing.

Family folklore is both traditional and evolving. It belongs to the entire family, to all the branches in the family tree, and everyone participates in it. Each generation forgets or changes the stories told by the previous generation and, at the same time, adds new stories and lore. In our modern times, with its rapid social and technological change, we might believe the previous generation lived in an entirely different historical era. Yet the lessons of their stories can still have great value to the newer generations.

Collecting family folklore can be a daunting project that could require direct and wide-ranging family engagement. To be practical, you might want to collect, frame, and tell stories from limited sources to share with your closest family members. Even so, preserving past stories is only half the picture. You'll need to keep your eyes, ears, and mind open to record the stories and lore as they are unfolding. New traditions are as valid as those that have existed for generations. So, even if your focus is just your branch of the family tree and is limited to those family members who live nearby, you'll need to develop a manageable approach: how to organize lore from the past as well as new traditions and stories from an ever-changing present.

Creating

Whether your search for family folklore is extensive or limited, the best place to begin is with yourself. As you reflect on your own family memories and how to retrieve them as stories, you'll increase your ability to recall them in greater detail. You'll develop a sense of remembered place and people, enhanced sensory images, and clarity of dialogue. Once you connect to the story-making process, you'll be more able to guide other family members in interviews and recordings.

Unavoidably, you'll develop your unique point of view and your own historical perspective on family events. But be aware that your impressions are only the starting point. Family members can often have an entirely different take on the same event and widely divergent opinions of a family member.

Nevertheless, continue to begin with your own memories and refine them in an ongoing process:

- Stretch your family memories into past decades
- Open your mind to new perspectives
- Test your information or interview relatives to verify
- Identify your gaps in information

- Collect new generational stories
- Become aware of new traditions today

Your ultimate goal is to become a more or less neutral eyewitness to the family stories of the past and those unfolding in front of your eyes.

For example, as I began to think of myself as an eyewitness to family experiences, I remembered a time when I did just that:

> My father brought home a fancy pair of binoculars from the military base and left them out on a living room table. I was just a skinny, six-year-old girl, but I grabbed them, sat on the floor in a hidden corner of the room, and adjusted the focus of the lenses. Fascinated, I watched the family's everyday action magnified and started to describe them out loud in a running commentary, like the voiceover in a documentary: "There's my daddy, he just walked through the room, looking for my little brother who's crying somewhere. Oh, Daddy found him out in the backyard, and now he's carrying Johnny back inside." Then I'd follow his movements with the binoculars, like I was panning with a movie camera. I kept that up for a while until Daddy got annoyed and said, "Katie, stop that!" It must have been unnerving.

Imagine yourself as a fly on the wall—a poised camera lens—and report what is taking place with as much real, authentic detail as possible as you relive a family story. Notice the time of day, the year, and the season of your event. Be alert, and take the time to seek out new information while conjuring family memories. Once focused, you'll be surprised what comes to mind.

As you retrieve family memories and shape them into stories, you will not be able to escape a personal point of view. Some stories will simply be yours to tell. Others can be more neutral, a retelling of a story your mother told about your grandfather, for instance. In that case, you become a more objective narrator. Nevertheless, each story needs to contain the essential story elements:

- Setting
- Characters
- Conflict, tension, suspense
- Narrative arc of rising action, increasing tension
- Sensory images within the action
- Dialogue within the action
- Resolution of tension, conclusion

As I searched my memory for a family folklore story, I found myself thinking of a person, place, or thing most family members would recognize across generations. I thought about the items in the storage boxes kept in a rented storage unit: the family archives. The one object that surfaced in my mind's eye was a wooden stable sign for one of Grandfather Fischer's racehorses from the 1940s. We'd passed that sign around from house to house and kept it as a token of his champion racehorse—a good luck charm better than a horseshoe. Lingering on the mental image of the bright green stable sign, I remembered when I saw that racehorse win, one summer's day—and the story took shape.

Folklore frequently contains a little bit of wonder and magic. This story has some of those elements, but above all, it is an

empowering story and a confidence-builder, a good one to add
to the family's patchwork quilt.

Katie F.

My grandfather owned racehorses—not for the big time,
and not even with a jockey. His sport was harness racing:
horses pulled a two-wheeled cart called a sulky with a
driver. Grandfather raced in county fairs around the Midwest
starting in the 1920s. Grandmother said he would not give
up his horses in the Great Depression and sacrificed all else
to keep them.

One summer in the late 1940s, my family visited our
grandparents in Kewanee, Illinois, when I was eight years
old and my older brother ten. We found treasures in the
attic, trophies of all the many wins, silver- and gold-plated
loving cups, mounted horses, and platters. By that time,
Grandfather had named a horse for each grandchild. But the
one horse who was the runaway champion was named for
me, Katie F. We were eager to see her race—and win.

At last, the day came; my brother and I rode with our
grandparents to the county fair in Princeton, Illinois, to see
the horse races and watch Katie F. We climbed up the stairs
of the white, wooden grandstand and watched her race on
the dusty, oval racing track, rounding the bend, one time,
two times, and finally coming around the bend on the home
stretch. We were jumping up and down in the bleacher
seats, banging loudly, yelling over and over, "Come on,
Katie F!" She came nearer to the stands and the finish line—
in the lead. And she won! We shrieked.

After the race, I wandered away from the family to the
stables. I searched for my horse by her stable sign, painted
in gold letters on bright green, Katie F. She leaned out of
the half door and I came closer, awestruck. I admired her
shining, chestnut-brown coat, the powerful muscles of a
standardbred. She towered over me. I dared not touch her
outstretched nose but came closer. She seemed to look right
at me, and I heard her say without a sound, "You do that."

I knew she meant for me to be like her, to win my race. She was my totem, my namesake.

After all these years, the only object that survived my grandfather's horseracing is that wooden stable sign: Katie F. It has traveled from place to place, kept by different family members. Katie F. is our legend, the great-hearted spirit of a winner.

Crafting

To set the stage for this family story, I researched a few details of harness racing, an old-fashioned sport, now almost nonexistent on racing tracks in the United States. But it had an exotic history in the ancient world: Assyrian kings in 1500 BCE maintained elaborate stables and professional trainers for horses used to draw chariots. There were four-horse hitch chariot races in the Olympic Games of the seventh century BCE and races with two-horse hitches earlier. Modern harness racing declined with the road horse, the advent of the car, and auto racing.

Even as a child, harness racing seemed glamorous to me. I felt that Katie F. (F for Fischer) and the other pacers were a prouder breed. No jockey ever rode them, saddled them, or whipped them into a frenzy. The gait of harness racing was stylized, and it could never be broken during a race. The pacing horse, or pacer, moved both legs on one side of its body at the same time, so they appeared to be dancing to a fast rhythm—at least to my eyes.

Though none of this research entered my story per se, it gave
my understanding of harness racing more authority and
added to my appreciation of the horses who raced—of their
mastery and strength. Horseracing in and of itself is a risky
undertaking. The suspense in this story is the anticipation
of seeing if our champion, Katie F., would win her race, if we
would be there to see her win, and how it would affect us.

**Researching the history of harness racing enhanced
my memories of that day, the race, and the impressive
athleticism of the champion winner, Katie F.**

Layers of Meaning

It was a surprise to discover how much that one horse race at a
county fair in the summer of my eighth year meant to me and
possibly to the entire Fischer family. That a champion horse
with my name would become a motivator and an influencer
throughout my life still seems odd, since I only witnessed
one race and visited her stall that one time. But Katie F. was
bigger than life, and she assumed a presence in our family: a
wonder horse—an expression of my grandfather's love of us. I
realized that:

- Animals and pets are part of the family

- Animals can transcend their lifetimes

- Animals can communicate

- Special, emblematic animals can become spirit guides

- Heirlooms can become totems or power objects

It would be effective to tell this story with the wooden stable sign and to pass it around to the group, along with any other memorabilia of Grandfather's horseracing days: photos, news articles, and horse blankets. Inviting other family members to share their memories about Grandfather as a horse racer and breeder would extend the storytelling experience in a natural, traditional way.

Telling

As you tell a family folklore story, you might discover that other family members will add details or dispute them. Each telling will help you discover the core of the story—its basic truth that most family members can accept. The more you reflect on the wider meaning of the tale, the more likely it will survive as folklore.

Once you've developed a clear narrative arc for the family story, simplify its format to a bare-bones outline. In this way, you'll be able to vary its telling, including making it longer or shorter, without memorizing it.

Outline the story, stripping details down to keywords and indicating its narrative arc.

For example, here is an outline of "Katie F."

1. Setting: Grandfather Fischer, harness racing in the Midwest, Illinois

2. Characters: Grandparents, grandchildren, racehorses

3. First scene: Rising action, attic filled with trophies, anticipation of the champion's race

4. Second scene: Rising action, county fair, grandstand, racetrack, cheering, winning

5. Third scene: Conclusion, stables, Katie F., message to win

6. Resolution: Stable sign, legacy

Use the outline to practice telling the story, and store your notes in a digital or print folder. For family stories like this one, you might want to tape it as an audio or video recording. It's possible to set up a private YouTube account for family viewing, a simple website, or a series of podcasts.

In Chapter Four, you'll discover other ways to structure the story outline using a storyboard, story map, or mind map. You'll also find tips for effective delivery.

The "Seven Steps to Storytelling" were original to the Word Weaving Storytelling Project and featured throughout its highly successful, professional trainings for educators. These demystify the art of storytelling into easy-to-learn steps.

Exercises & Prompts: Family Folklore

Memory Triggers

- Photos, keepsakes, jewelry, and other objects can be productive memory triggers

- Photo albums and memorabilia at relatives' homes can stimulate stories

- Visits to a neighborhood or city where you or the family once lived

- Touring the old stomping grounds: take notes, take photos, or record your thoughts

- Think of your favorite family recipe

Family Members as Resources

- Consult relatives to help round out your memories of a person or event into a full story

- Record family stories and exchanges of memories during family gatherings using audio or video

- Note conversational fragments and raw material to develop a full-fledged story

- Remember a story that was passed down from one generation to another

- Recall an event that your parents or guardians told you about

- Think of a story you heard about your childhood that you never forgot

- What is the story everyone in your family knows?

- Remember a story your grandparents, aunts, uncles, or elders told

Let all these memories and stories play in your mind's eye as you search for one story to tell. Select one that has a clear structure with a beginning, middle, and end. Choose one that has a conflict, a problem, suspense, tension, or an adventure.

Keep track of your process in whatever media is best suited to you: notebooks, digital files, recorded segments, or a scrapbook. As you collect material, develop an organizational system. It could be a simple timeline or a list of family members. It could even be a theme that defines the family folklore as you see it.

Storytellers Share Secrets: Family Folklore

Family folklore provides rich content for stories that can be used for performances on stage, at intimate family gatherings, or on a first date. Every family has stories that run the gamut from hilarious to courageous to tragic. We have the option to choose what best suits our audience. Sometimes we might tell one to family members who've heard the story before but want to hear it again newly told or want to share it with new family members.

These two storytellers tell humorous family stories that depict the lively nature of family folklore— how it travels and changes as families move across boundaries.

Creating

Author and storyteller **Claire Hennessy** moved from the UK to live in California in 2008, the shock of which propelled her to start writing as a form of cheap therapy. She is a founding member of Write on Mamas, a San Francisco Bay Area writing group. She has been published in four anthologies, including the award-winning *She's Got This: Essays on Standing Strong and Moving On* and *Nothing But the Truth So Help Me God— Transitions*. She has performed at Lit Quake, Lit Crawl, The Moth, The Marsh, and other storytelling events and venues.

Family Folklore

Claire Hennessy

How do I select a story? I like to tell funny stories, so I start there. What memories make me laugh or cringe? Embarrassment is a prime factor in selecting my subject matter. I also speak to my family, particularly my two sisters. I jot down incidents in a notebook. Then I write down the pertinent facts, normally in the form of bullet points. I try to figure out the main story plot and unique features. What makes it different from anyone else's story? What makes it humorous?

Once I have all the details at hand, I open up a new Word document and just start typing. I try to type as if I were telling the story to someone else. Sometimes I pretend to do this by speaking out loud and recording myself on my phone and then transcribing it. When I have finished a first draft, I leave it for a while, usually overnight. Often, when I come back to it, I see things that I didn't write clearly enough, or I think of a funnier way to say something. I also read it out loud again as this can highlight where sentences are too long or the structure is awkward.

Claire's process for selecting and creating a story to be spoken is an excellent one. She is aware that her ultimate goal is to tell her family story live on stage to an eager audience of listeners. Though her aim is to entertain, her creative process clearly shows the need to be authentic and to build a story plot with unique, appealing features. Consulting with family members adds to the truth of the story and to her confidence in telling it. Keeping her audience as the primary focus ensures that her story successfully adapts to spoken word presentation. Working from incident to bullet points to free write to audio recording and back to a final script reflects her professionalism as a storyteller. We can already hear the applause.

Crafting

Birthday Traditions

Claire Hennessy

In my family, we love to celebrate. Christmas, anniversaries, and special achievements (such as weight loss or a good hair day), but above all, we love celebrating birthdays. Over the years, we have developed a few slightly strange traditions.

Firstly, on the morning of the birthday, we call and sing "Happy Birthday" in the most out-of-tune, off-key way possible—starting high, going low, warbling painfully, followed by loud cackling laughter. It is not a pleasant experience for the listener, which is the whole point. This probably started as none of us had a good singing voice.

I'll give you an idea of how bad my voice is. When my son was a toddler, I took him to a mother and baby group. At the end, mothers sat in a circle with their children on their laps and sang a few nursery rhymes. One time, I forgot to mime. My son turned around and firmly placed a pudgy hand over my mouth, much to the amusement of everyone present. It has become such a habit for me to sing in this pantomime fashion that people from other countries have actually thought it is an eccentric, ancient British tradition and have tried to emulate it!

As if this singing tradition wasn't embarrassing enough, our mother insisted on making her children cut birthday cakes in a rather peculiar way. We were told to hold the knife upside down (so we were using the blunt edge) and force the knife through whatever birthday cake was in front of us—hopefully not a homemade one, as that was not my mum's forte—straining our puny muscles, while at the same time screaming loudly and making a wish. She told us that if we didn't do all these things together, our wishes wouldn't come true! This was particularly humiliating when celebrating publicly in a restaurant. She never explained why and has since denied all knowledge.

Strangely, despite my childhood mortification, I dutifully passed on these traditions to my kids, to their deep displeasure.

This is such a delicious family story: it exhibits both self-deprecating humor and self-pride. As Claire honors the eccentricities of her family's birthday traditions, she seems to showcase their inexplicable brilliance. Claire uses sensory detail to create a full experience: the sounds of singing are brought to life with descriptive adjectives, and the ritual cutting of the cake with attention-grabbing verbs, like "force" and "screaming." We feel the truth of her traditions in how detailed they are and the emotional tone that is present throughout the stories.

With two traditions told in sequence, we become aware of their intrinsic family lore and underlying culture. One tradition builds on the other in a way that heightens their effect, builds suspense, and entertains. That Claire passed these humiliating birthday traditions on to her own children is the final, satisfying conclusion: their audacious creativity celebrated. It's a great example of the wry British sense of humor.

Creating

Humaira Ghilzai is a writer, speaker, and a consultant on the culture of Afghanistan. Humaira opens the world to Afghan culture and cuisine through her popular blog, *Afghan Culture Unveiled*. She shares the wonders of Afghanistan through stories of rich culture, delicious food, and her family's traditions. Humaira's writing has been published in *Encore Magazine, Mataluna: A Book of 152 Afghan Pashto Proverbs,* and *Medium.*

Humaira Ghilzai

Stories, like photos, are best told at a close range. I pick stories that not only have meaning for me, but that also impart a piece of my Afghan culture to the reader. My writing process is not organic, inspirational, or euphoric. My first hour of writing is spent on social media, the *New York Times* website, and various other distractions. Once I start feeling guilty, I set the Tomato Timer on my iPhone to twenty-five minutes; I grab hold of a pen and start writing in my notebook. Sometimes I get nonsense and other times gems. Depending on the length of what I'm writing, I may repeat this self-imposed discipline a couple times more.

After I have enough material, I reward myself with a cup of cardamom tea before typing everything into my computer, editing as I go. This is the start of a lengthy editing process during which my husband, a reluctant but thorough editor, reads the piece after I've ironed out many of the kinks. He usually tears apart what I have written, and then I go into another round of edits.

I've tried outlining pieces, but in general, what works best for me is mulling over a piece in my head while I go for a walk or when I'm cooking. I basically form a structure for the story before I sit down for the free write. However, nothing can replace the process of editing, especially with a trusted editor's input.

Humaira invites us into her home for a cup of tea as she shares her personal process for creating a story, one she hopes will highlight aspects of Afghan culture. She writes with a system of immediate rewards and enjoys an in-house editor. Beginning with a basic story structure and expanding it with a number of free writes and several drafts, she disciplines herself in timed segments. It's obvious that Humaira has a strong voice in her writing, and she readily connects to the reader—we are immediately drawn in. Her humor is another lovely gift; it further engages the audience as she shares her foibles with us.

Crafting

How My Afghan Family Saved Christmas

Humaira Ghilzai

I think back to 1998, when my husband Jim and I hosted our first Christmas holiday get-together. Although I had spent a couple of holidays with Jim's family, I had never played hostess. Looking back, Christmas dinner was a little over my head. Come to think of it, there were several things wrong with this plan:

1. I didn't celebrate Christmas growing up.

2. I did not know how to cook.

3. I had no idea what one traditionally serves on Christmas.

After consulting Jim, who turned out to know less than I did, I made a game day plan—fresh bagels, lox, and cream cheese from the bagel shop down the street on Christmas morning. For Christmas dinner, I called an upscale grocery store nearby and ordered the full line-up: "homemade" turkey, stuffing, potatoes, rolls, vegetables, and dessert.

On Christmas morning, as I turned onto Fillmore Street, I realized that every shop on the street was closed, including the bagel shop. To my horror, I realized that *everything* was closed on Christmas. Not just the bagel shop, but the grocers, too. I ran home and shook Jim awake.

"Did you know everything is closed on Christmas day?" I asked.

"Yes, everyone knows that," he said.

Everyone, apparently, except me. Panicked, I called my mom, who was appalled at the thought that my in-laws would miss not one, but two meals under my watch. After a morning of fretting and wringing her hands, my mom called to say the family would be sending over their dinner for that night. At five thirty, my brother, Waheed, showed up at my doorstep with two roasted chickens, still warm, and several side dishes. Not knowing my Afghan mother's standards of hospitality, Jim's family was amazed that my family had given up their meal so we could have a special Christmas dinner.

Family folklore should be homey and inclusive: Humaira's story welcomes us into her family's Christmas with the tone of her first unassuming words. We experienced her holiday quandary with her: how could a newly wedded Afghan woman host her husband's American family on Christmas day? Her choice of title says it all: She needed an Afghan village to host her in-laws.

Even though Humaira emigrated with her family when she was eleven as they sought asylum from the Soviet invasion, she had not experienced the American traditions of Christmas. Her family had enjoyed time off work and the post-holiday sales, but they hadn't exchanged gifts. Her lack of understanding is a great setup for how her careful meal planning ended up being thwarted. In her panicked phone call to her mother, we see not only Humaira's immediate dilemma, but the cultural one as well. For her Afghan family, not treating honored guests generously would bring shame—to their province, clan, and qala (the family compound) as well as to their family. The blending of these two traditions on Christmas day is a wonderful story: it shows how family folklore changes as families move.

Family Secrets and Shadows

There's nothing louder than a family secret—it pesters and pokes until someone speaks up. Secrets have a way of hiding in plain sight. There are always the whispered rumors, the missing pieces of a puzzle, the stories that keep changing. But just as shared family folklore can develop strength and identity, keeping family secrets can destroy trust. Secrets that persist, unspoken and misunderstood, can erode the very foundation of a family. Family members who are perceptive, who sense hidden truths, may become fearful or internalize guilt and shame. At the very least, family secrets isolate—they isolate family members from one another and the entire family from their community.

Some family secrets are more harmful to keep than others. Those that were traumatic, that violated some taboo, or that were life-changing are vital to expose. Some of these important secrets can only be shared privately, within the family, and only with members old enough to understand. Certainly, by the time most children reach adulthood, they ought to know most of the essential family secrets that were kept from them yet influenced their lives in ways both known and unknown.

As Suzanne Handler, mental health educator and author of *The Secrets They Kept*, cautions:

> Keeping secrets within a family can create a false sense of reality, especially among children. When eventually told the truth, either by a parent, or, even worse, by someone outside the family, their world may feel shattered. Secrets' impact on children can be profound, regardless of their age. Parents who habitually keep secrets from their children

should keep in mind the possibility that such behavior could very well be repeated in future generations.

When considering the sensitive nature of family secrets, a storyteller should proceed with care. There will be those in the family who will never accept the truth, even once it is exposed. Yet there will be those members who will feel relieved or validated by newly discovered stories that make sense of a puzzle. It can be a powerful healing process for many. Of course, there will also be relatives who find family secrets fascinating and telling them juicy entertainment. As a family member and storyteller, it's often a challenge to share family secrets in a responsible but enduring way.

Secrets make the best stories. In fiction, secrets can provide motivation, plot, character, even a setting. From *Madame Bovary* to *Carrie*, from *Rebecca* to *Big Little Lies*, from thrillers to romance, from mystery to women's fiction to sci-fi, stories frequently revolve around secrets. A good number of book blurbs contain the word, "secret." Secrets are tantalizing to the reader and create a supercharged plot for the writer. Family secrets take starring roles in women's fiction and in memoir. To sell a book, there's nothing better than a "deeply buried family secret."

How does the storyteller make use of this powerful plot twist: the revelation of closely held and defended secrets? As with family folklore, it's best to begin with yourself and your own need to tell a family secret—if only to your immediate family. It's a good place to start: secrets ripple outward through the generations, and, whenever they are told, they begin to dissipate.

Creating

As you ponder what secrets you've learned about your family, either from relatives or from research, choose the ones whose revealed truth meant the most to you. Which ones contributed most to your identity and resolved issues that once confused you? Select the ones with the most personal impact to shape into stories to tell, to store in notebooks, or to record. As you share these, other family members might be encouraged to share theirs.

For example, my family had more than its share of secrets. Even as a very young child, I wondered at the oddities of my parents: why did we move so often, and why did we live so far away from the rest of our relatives? Because my mother didn't know why and was confused for over a decade and then because she was sworn to absolute secrecy, I did not begin to understand the reason until I was in my mid-thirties. Years later, I continued to uncover how far-reaching the hidden truth had been. Indeed, this scandalous secret irrevocably shaped my childhood and that of my two brothers.

The secret: When my parents married in the Catholic Church in 1939, my father was aware that he was gay at a time when it was a criminal offense to be a homosexual in most states. With others' advice, Dad made the decision to pretend to be straight, marry, and shelter himself within a family. This particular family secret was *buried* for decades. It was definitely central to my life story, to my childhood family, and to those close to us. That it did not surface until there was no criminal consequence for my father's sexual preference was chilling. No doubt, there were reasons to keep it quiet—but there was also denial. My father passed away years ago, at peace with himself and his life. How to tell the family story now?

For a family secret to stand on its own and tell its story, it should have at least three parts in a clear narrative arc:

- Beginning: Scenes when the secret created tension and conflict, when it had the most impact

- Revelation: Scenes when the secret was partially or fully revealed over time

- Resolution: Scenes of the truth and explanation, acceptance or denial of it

Each scene in the story needs to contain essential story elements:

- Setting

- Characters

- Sensory images within the action

- Dialogue within the action

As I thought about my dad's secret and how it had shaped all of us without our knowing it, I remembered Dad's first cousin, Bill. Bill shared the same secret as Dad but chose a different life path. Yet both cousins lived in the shadows.

The Deli: Cold Case

Back when I was a graduate student in San Francisco in the early '60s, my grandmother sent me a letter all the way from Kewanee, Illinois. "Why don't you look up your cousin

Bill?" she wrote. "He's my sister Ida's son and works in a grocery store there, Grand Central Market."

I wrote back, saying I sure would, since that was *my* grocery store, just two blocks down the hill on California Street at the corner of Fillmore, a swank spot. I was excited to meet him and planned to invite him for a visit. I wondered why I'd never heard of Bill, but my dad rarely spoke of his relatives—he kept his distance.

I found Bill behind the deli counter, a massive white case filled with expensive delicacies for the Pacific Heights socialites who lived farther up Fillmore. He looked so much like my dad, with his bright, cornflower blue eyes, turned-up nose, and lean face. The sparkle in his eyes reminded me of my elfin grandmother, his aunt.

But when he visited along with his partner, Don, our friendship had a chilly end. Don sat in the living room with his slicked-back, thinning, dark hair, glaring at me and my artist roommate, Nancy, making sure we knew that he was in charge—the manager of the store and evidently of Bill. Bill barely spoke, and he glanced helplessly around the sparsely furnished room. My roommate and I got the message.

We whispered to each other after they left, "Do you think they're, you know, homosexuals?" My hip roommate said, "Wow, that guy Don doesn't want you anywhere near your cousin."

Later, when I shopped at Grand Central, I would stop by the deli counter just to say hello. We'd steal a few glances, Bill sending me wordless apologies—his blue eyes full of regret. I moved on from the neighborhood, keeping their secret, while Bill and Don prospered in that upscale store. I was glad for Bill, until I chanced to read his obituary in the May 1993, *Marin Independent Journal*: No known survivors. No service. Burial in Kewanee, Illinois.

Oh, Bill, my heart is full of regret.

Crafting

Shaping my brief encounter with my cousin Bill into a story
was a healing process for me. I visualized the moments
of contact, magnified in my mind's eye: the details of the
grocery store and the enormous deli counter, its cold case
an impenetrable barrier. I recalled Bill's eyes; they were so
expressive, from delight at meeting me, to nervous glances,
and finally his painful gaze across the glass counter. Bill didn't
have to speak; I understood his anxiety. There was too much at
risk—his secret life, his relationship, his financial well-being.
Those reasons I did respect, while my grandmother remained
oblivious. I also realized that my sense of the loss of my cousin
was ever-present. As I ended this story, I became aware that
acknowledging Bill and the loneliness of his passing was a way
forward to a healing and a final acceptance of his life choices.

A brief internet search filled in the gaps and helped me to
understand more about Bill's life. I learned that during World
War II he was a warrant officer in the US Army, a highly
trained specialist assigned to the Presidio in Monterey, CA.
I could speculate that it was there he had met his partner,
discovered the underground community of gay men in San
Francisco, and begun to work in the grocery business after the
war. I knew that while Bill had died alone and without a will,
he had been a wealthy man. Grand Central Market remained
a San Francisco landmark, a high-end store in an increasingly
gentrified neighborhood. When the market was purchased by
a new franchise, Mollie Stone's Markets, the original Grand

Central Market sign was not removed—a nod to the fine old market, and secretly, also to Bill.

This research provided more depth to Bill's life, so I could tell this story with the confidence and acceptance that came from knowing his considerable achievements.

Layers of Meaning

In selecting this family secret and giving it a title, I discovered that pain still existed in the thwarted relationship between me and my cousin. The resentment that we could not be friendly, not even in our own neighborhood, began to lessen as I created the ending. As I continue to tell this family secret and introduce our cousin to other family members, healing can occur. This story meant a great deal to me; it allowed me to:

- Remember my cousin who lived in self-imposed isolation nearby

- Relive the loss of his kinship

- Honor his memory and life choices

- Celebrate his successes and service

- Compare his life choices to those of my father, his first cousin

- Acknowledge the intense bond of family

Sharing this story in a family gathering might lead to further conversations about how to value all family members, how to reach out to those in the shadows, and how to celebrate the unique qualities of each relative and his or her intrinsic worth.

We might also discuss the ongoing struggles of the LGBTQ community and how those issues continue to affect our family.

Telling

Family secrets have lasting consequences. As you uncover those most important to your legacy, you'll discover their enduring outcomes; your understanding of the family dynamic will deepen. Not least among your perceptions will be the effect the revealed story has on other family members. Some will remain in denial. Your sensitivity in knowing when and how to share this story will become one of its essential components.

As with all written drafts, reduce the sequence of action to a simple outline. In this way, you'll be able to tell the story without memorizing it, and you can add details appropriate to your listeners.

Outline the story, stripping details down to keywords and indicating its narrative arc.

For example, here is an outline of "The Deli: Cold Case."

1. Setting: San Francisco neighborhood, Lower Pacific Heights, 1960s, apartment, grocery

2. Characters: My cousin Bill, his partner Don, my roommate Nancy, me

3. First scene: Rising action, meeting my cousin

4. Second scene: Rising action, my cousin and partner visiting my apartment

5. Third scene: Stolen glances at the deli

6. Resolution: Bill's passing, my regrets

Retain the story outline with your family memories in a digital file or print folder along with photos or other documents. This is a story that might be more closely held, though no longer hidden.

You might also want to use the structural tools and tips in Chapter Four to shape your story for telling, such as a story map or mind map, as well as a storyboard.

The "Seven Steps to Storytelling" were original to the Word Weaving Storytelling Project and featured throughout its highly successful, professional trainings for educators. These demystify the art of storytelling into easy-to-learn steps.

Exercises & Prompts:
Family Secrets & Shadows

Prompts: Shadows

1. Think of a family member in the past who was shunned or forgotten

2. Remember someone who brought shame to the family

3. Recall a family member in past generations who committed a wrong

4. Remember someone who was wrongly accused

5. Think of a family member who was judged by an outdated taboo

6. Remember a relative who was flawed or found lacking

7. Think of a time when you were judged or the family thought less of you: what happened?

Prompts: Secrets

1. What are the worst family secrets?

2. Which misdeeds were committed three or four generations back?

3. What secrets were kept by your grandparents' generation?

4. What secrets were kept by your parents' generation?

5. What secrets were yours or your siblings'?

6. Are there secrets still hidden by your family today?

7. What secrets of yours do you want to share with your family?

Let all these memories and stories play in your mind's eye as you search for one story to tell. Select one that has a clear structure with a beginning, middle, and end. Choose one that has a conflict, a problem, suspense, tension, or an adventure.

Keep track of your process in whatever media is best suited to you: notebooks, digital files, recorded segments, or a scrapbook. As you collect material, develop an organizational system. It could be a simple timeline or a list of family members.

Storytellers Share Secrets:
Family Secrets & Shadows

Family secrets and family members who remained in the shadows exert more influence than you might think. What is repressed has its own way of surfacing and may do so in unknown ways. By giving voice to the hushed stories, you can add more substance to the entire family. If done with empathy and compassion, the family can begin to accept what was once shunned and heal. These storytellers have found this to be true by opening the door to the past and releasing its disgrace.

Creating

Marlene Cullen is enthusiastic about encouraging people to write, even those who think they can't. Her series of books, The Write Spot anthologies, feature writing that entertains as well as inspires other writers. Marlene is the founder of Writers Forum of Petaluma, a monthly literary event featuring presenters talking about the craft and business of writing. Marlene's award-winning short stories and essays have been published in literary journals, anthologies, and newspapers, including *Tiny Lights*, *Building Bridges*, *More Bridges*, the Redwood Writers anthologies, and The Write Spot anthologies.

The Free Write Style of Writing

Marlene Cullen

I am passionate about free writes, a way of writing freely, letting words tumble out and letting them fall however they land, with no thoughts or worries about the outcome. The free write method is an opportunity to explore and play with writing. Ideas burst out during this unique type of writing. Free writes can also offer ideas for future writing.

With free writes, personal experiences emerge for your writing, or you can write about something that happened to someone else. If you are writing fiction, you can respond to the prompt the way your fictional character would respond. Writing prompts can be used to inspire writing. Prompts can be a word, a phrase, a picture, a sound, a smell, or a line from a book or a poem. Set a timer for fifteen minutes to corral your writing time. Choose a prompt and start writing.

Free writes, or stream-of-consciousness writing, may reveal new thoughts and perhaps uncover information and present answers that haven't been previously discovered. I reached an epiphany about my father after several free writes.

Marlene employs the practice of free writing, or "free writes," with great success and has shared it with many writers over the years. It is also called timed writing, and the results are unpredictable, creative, and at times, surprising. It's one sure way to reach into the shadows of one's memory to gain insight into a family member whose status in the family was diminished, as Marlene does with her father. By letting her mind probe a theme without judgement, she reveals her own feelings, ones she's kept under wraps for a lifetime. Start, as Marlene does, with a prompt about family secrets and see where your free writing takes you. Use a free write to explore the secrets and shadows within your own family.

Crafting

Meeting My Father

Marlene Cullen

I have always had a hard time describing how my father didn't fit into our family. He was a merchant seaman who was away from home for months. He brought home exotic toys and clothes for me and my sisters, always too small.

"I have the perfect family: a daddy, a mommy, and two little girls." I knew I wasn't telling the truth to my second-grade playmates, but if I pretended hard enough, maybe it would come true.

When my father was home, it meant he was out of work and could be found at one neighborhood bar or another. I have a child's handful of memories about my father—none of them are good. The best I could say was that he was a "Third Street Bum." He died when he was thirty-seven of alcohol-related diseases. I was sixteen.

When I was fifty-four, through a series of serendipitous happenings, I met my father's high school best friends. They painted a picture of him as a happy-go-lucky kid. They said Bill was a quiet guy, a gentleman, a prankster, and very sensitive. Seeing my father through the eyes of his teenage friends introduced me to the person I never knew.

Sloshing my way through free writes, I realized my father was more than a person with an alcohol problem. He was a husband and a father, a loving son, and a loyal friend struggling to navigate the challenges of life.

Several free writes about my father evolved into a story revealing my epiphany about him, one that was published in *The Write Spot: Memories*. My insight concludes: "He is a part of me, imperfections as well as the good parts. He is part of my granddaughter, who shares his hazel-colored eyes." Without free writes, my father would have remained a "lesser" person in my mind.

It's a credit to Marlene that she is willing to open up to a new understanding of her father, a parent her family had written off as a deadbeat dad. That she used the writing skill she's taught many others demonstrates her desire to reach back into a repressed past. Marlene knew that a free write would accomplish her goal: She would finally meet her father as she continued to write. One part of her success is her intention of finding him; another is the way her free writing practice accesses new information contained in memories. Free writing fosters free association: one fragment or memory leads to another.

Creating

KJ Landis is an author, educator, and health and life coach. She holds a bachelor of science degree in education and has certificates in personal training, Pilates, and fitness class instruction, as well as continuing education certifications in psychology, childhood development, and nutrition. KJ Landis has written numerous books on wellness. Her weekly videos and blogs share information on holistic health topics as well as providing motivational and inspirational support.

KJ Landis

My unique process for telling a personal story is to take acting workshops, especially improvisational workshops. My favorite writing mentor is focused on teaching students how to write and perform one-woman and one-man shows. We do lots of movement and vocal exercises and then are given a writing prompt. We write for ten to twelve minutes and share our personal stories aloud to each other in a safe space—meaning that we promise to keep all shared content inside the room. Combining acting with writing allows us to experience more facets of who we are and what we want to share with others. It also helps us home in on our impact upon others through sharing our personal narratives.

How does one choose which personal memory to write about? Choose one that is vivid: one you remember in every detail. Choose one with a lot at stake for you. Every memory has a beginning, middle, and end that also has conflict inside of it. It doesn't have to be a struggle; it only has to be meaningful enough to remember all these years later.

KJ Landis's process is similar in some ways to Marlene's free writes in that KJ uses prompts and timed writings that lead to an open-ended exploration of memories. KJ further stimulates the story-making process with the techniques of improvisation and body movement in acting workshops. A story comes alive when the teller is on her feet, working with other members of the group in an improvised scene. KJ probes the deeper emotional meaning of events to translate them into performance art. These techniques are particularly effective in working with traumatic experiences and buried memories, as well as releasing emotional pain. KJ's commitment to wellness in her work as a life coach motivates her to know and tell her life stories. By doing so and by embracing them fully, she is able to heal and to communicate the truth of her experiences through the art of storytelling.

Crafting

Date Night: Story Summary

KJ Landis

A young Jewish girl, age seven, the youngest of five children, I was born into a family of Eastern European and Russian immigrants. Yiddish was often spoken in our Pittsburgh home as a way to keep secrets from us children.

When I was a child, I adored my mother's beauty, her jewelry, her fancy party clothing, her cooking and baking skills, and her bedtime storytelling. She used to go out with my dad for ballroom dancing and dinner at a fancy supper club, and I used to help her get ready to go out. It was exciting to see how breathtaking she was at her exit from the house.

But something was lurking underneath for me. Fear. I really didn't want her to leave, because with every click, click, click of her high heels down the stairs toward the front door, I knew what would follow.

I wrote a piece about happened when my parents left the home on date nights and left us with the babysitters.

Let's just say it wasn't pretty or fun.

Look at me. Look at me. Look at me now. Look at me. I grew—I am growing. I had no choice but to survive. To survive is to thrive. Bubbling up just under the surface: it's there, always there. Memories bubble up just under my sweater, seeping through my skin. I have no choice.

In this story summary, meant to be told aloud rather than read, KJ reveals a secret that is all too often kept hidden, both in families and in our society. Sexual abuse of children is only now coming into the public eye. Yet these experiences are traumatic and cause lasting damage. KJ's skill as a storyteller is evident in how she frames this story from the beginning: Yiddish is spoken by her parents to keep secrets from the children. The irony of this opening statement is clear by the end of the story: the children have devastating secrets they keep from their parents.

KJ builds suspense as she describes her mother's beauty and the glamor of her date night with her father. The sensory images are vivid: the click, click, of her mother's high heels as she leaves. These few specific details bring us into the story of her remembered experience. Though KJ does not say explicitly what happened on her parents' date nights, we know—her last images are tactile. What is powerful about the story's ending is a repeated phrase that shifts from past tense to present tense: "I *had* no choice; I *have* no choice." In the end, KJ tells us that her choice is to live and to thrive, even with painful memories ever-present.

Family secrets and shadows, when kept in the dark, weaken the family's foundation. By telling them in a responsible way to family members who are mature enough to hear them, you can release their negative hold. The truth can set your family free: by accepting their secrets, members of a family are more able to accept one another with compassion. Telling family secrets through stories is a powerful and compelling art.

Family Legacy

Family legacy stories are the banner headlines of a family's storytelling tradition. They are the stories everyone seems to know, or at least recalls hearing. These oft-told tales convey powerful messages from those who came before us. It's a great benefit to realize that our families possess a literary legacy above and beyond mainstream culture—that we own a unique store of wisdom drawn from the ancestral experiences of our family. The impact of our legacy stories is with us, whether we fully recall the stories or not. If it's better to know them, it's even better to tell them—and tell them well.

Because we share the intimacy of family, knowing the lineage of our family's storytelling truths gives us a deeper connection to our roots. Our unique stories, the very particular experiences of our ancestors, give us an understanding of life that no other information can. We connect to these tales because they are so very personal; we feel the events close to the bone. No other family has exactly the same legacy stories, even if the truths are universal. These stories are empowering: they infuse us with strength when we hear them. **Family legacy stories can stabilize us in our rapidly changing modern era and give us the long view: a return to the far past that helps us to face the present and imagine the future.**

Legacy stories can often be similar to family folklore stories or family secrets. But legacy stories are viewed through another lens: they are a look at the lessons learned from past generations and how they connect to history. A legacy story typically has a historical context and has been passed down through the generations with a significant meaning. Such stories are intrinsic to family identity. Each legacy story has a memorable quality, either because it is dramatic or because it speaks to a core belief.

If we want to have an impact on future generations, then we will be successful if we pay special attention to family legacy stories and pass on their values and lessons through the art of storytelling, rather than by giving lectures or dire warnings.

Rachael Freed, founder of Life-Legacies and author of *Your Legacy Matters*, encourages families to identify and tell important legacy stories.

> As storytelling beings, we are captivated by stories, particularly those that are connected to us. Stories we write about our families—our ancestors, their values, and their time in history—enable our children to transcend time and space, to discover or rediscover their history, and to deepen their roots. Family stories also provide children with values that can influence their future.

Creating

Since legacy stories are an intrinsic part of a family's culture, you might know a fragment, but perhaps the entire story seems to be just out of reach. You might not be sure if the way you remember it is accurate. Consulting other family members or reading over family records will help to fill in the blanks. It would be best, however, to first begin with what you do remember or think you know. That gives you a basis from which to build by adding details, checking information, and creating the story with your own understanding.

For example, I remember my grandfather Stadler telling me one summer's day in the 1940s, while we were visiting his home in Pontiac, Illinois, how he was mistreated by his stepmother. I was likely six years old the day we sat outdoors in his landscaped garden. Though there were other grandchildren playing nearby, I distinctly recall Grandfather talking only to me, with intense eye contact and vivid gestures. He told me that when his stepmother punished him as a young boy, she would lock him in a room without food or water. When dinner time came, she would open the door to a very hungry child and hand him a bowl of water with a stone in the middle—instead of soup and bread. I was horrified.

Though that fragment was only a brief memory, it provided the emotional context for all the other stories about Grandfather's abusive childhood. That he'd told it to me directly gave me the full sense of it—in the way he had peered into my eyes to make sure I heard, and how he had gestured, showing the shape of the bowl. A youngster myself, I didn't know Grandfather's motivation, but I felt his misery. Keeping that subtext alive helped me to interpret the other tales of his life as an orphan, such as the one I've summarized below, "Shoemaker's Apprentice." This woeful tale is a legacy story of the Stadler family, one that is told and retold and that every grandchild and great-grandchild has heard.

Selecting a legacy story is a simple process due to its prominence in the family's tradition. Keep in mind the key features of a legacy story:

- An ancestral tale of past generations, two or three generations back

- Origin of stories, including a variety or combination of sources if possible: word of mouth, research, primary source materials, such as newspapers, archives, historical societies

- Place in history: connection to the wider social context, of historical note

- Lessons conveyed, either explicit or implicit wisdom central to the family culture

- Audience: a story the new generation needs to hear or understand

With these criteria in mind, I selected and retold Grandfather Stadler's legacy story. It is a relevant story today, with current US immigration policy controversies and the dubious treatment of unaccompanied minors who are sponsored by relatives already in the US.

Shoemaker's Apprentice

About the end of the nineteenth century, an orphan boy, ragged and thin, wandered the cobblestone streets of Munich, the largest city in the kingdom of Bavaria in Germany. In spite of his small size and sickly cough, he went house to house begging for old shoes and leather. This boy was my grandfather, Ludwig Heinrich Stadler, who was apprenticed to a shoemaker at age ten. He was often sent to scavenge scraps of leather for shoe repairs. Unwanted, a burden to their large family, young Ludwig was first neglected by his stepparents, then they placed him as a child apprentice without even telling other relatives or his half-sister, Theresa.

On her Confirmation Day, Theresa's godparents took her to Munich to celebrate and have a special lunch. While in the fancy pastry shop enjoying her treat, Theresa saw a boy who looked like a street urchin with his face against the shop window, peering in at the delicious cakes and sweets.

"Oh, look at that poor boy," she said. "Why—that's Ludwig looking in the window!" She ran to hug her older brother. "What has happened to you? Your clothes are so dirty."

Her godparents came rushing outside. Sturdy folks, they gathered Ludwig up and took him inside the pastry shop, where he was served hot chocolate and warm food. Ludwig, gulping his thanks, told them where he was apprenticed, and he was soon glad to leave the shoemaker's workbench with his small bag of belongings.

On their return to the village of Tittling, Theresa's godparents sent word of Ludwig's weak condition to his surviving relatives. The Stadler family was in an uproar over Ludwig's harsh treatment. The starving boy was ill; in fact, he was consumptive.

"What have you done to this child!" They accused Ludwig's stepparents of child abuse—of stealing the money left for Ludwig and then selling him into apprenticeship.

Furious, his mother's relatives bundled Ludwig off to a monastery in Innsbruck, high in the Austrian Alps. There he was to recover in the mountain air, perhaps to become a priest. Ludwig worked in the large abbey kitchen and learned dietetics. By age fifteen, he'd grown strong enough to emigrate by steerage to a South Dakota ranch, sponsored by his aunt and uncle on his mother's side—a safe haven at last.

From Grandfather's story we learned of the blessing of godparents, the unbreakable bonds between mother and aunt as well as between Ludwig and his sister, resilience, stoicism, and survival.

Crafting

This story happened so long ago that I wanted it to sound like an old folktale, complete with cobblestoned streets in the kingdom of Bavaria. In fact, the European world order did not change until the armistice agreements after the first Great War. Ludwig's childhood seemed medieval to me in many ways.

I'd heard this legacy story from my mother, Ludwig's daughter; she'd heard it directly from his half-sister, Theresa. Once Ludwig arrived in South Dakota, he'd urged his aunt and uncle to sponsor his orphaned sister, concerned about her treatment at the hands of their stepparents. *Tante Trazel,* as she was known, became a schoolteacher and told this story about saving her brother to her many nieces and nephews. My mother, one of eight children, often told this tale when new members joined the family or at our family gatherings.

Ludwig's parentage and ethnic background has remained a mystery, although many family members attempted to discover the identity of his biological father. But we learned of both his mother's entire lineage in Bavaria and that of his first stepfather through genealogical work on the ground in Germany. Through dictated memories, letters, and US military documents, we found out that Ludwig signed up as a volunteer for military duty for the Spanish American War; he was assigned to the cavalry because of his experience as a South Dakota range rider and sent to the Philippines. Ludwig became a camp cook with General Pershing's forces in the Philippines and in Mexico during General Pershing's Pancho

Villa Expedition in 1916 to 1917. Ludwig was mustered out at the San Francisco Presidio in 1917.

In 1918, Ludwig took a state civil service examination for a position as a dietitian in the Illinois state penal system. Using his education at the abbey in Innsbruck, Austria, as well as his experience as camp cook in his military tours of duty with General Pershing, he qualified for the position. Ludwig worked as a dietitian in the Illinois prison system until retirement.

Ludwig continued to exist in harsh environments his whole life, from his childhood and his career at a monastery and a South Dakota ranch, to military expeditions and working in penitentiaries. In some ways, he never escaped the cruel conditions of his early years. Yet he was a nurturer to the men in those hard places as their cook.

This research provided more depth to Ludwig's life and to this legacy story. I could tell this story with confidence, knowing its origins and its context.

Layers of Meaning

This legacy story and its underlying facts uncovered by research, along with Grandfather's entire life story, are complex. The meaning it has for family members can vary widely, since it contains both powerful negative and positive influences.

- Stoicism and resilience
- Starvation and nurturance
- Orphan and patriarch
- Immigrant and patriot

Most family members rejoice at Ludwig's dramatic rescue and its positive consequences. Yet there was damage that could not be undone. Ludwig's legacy story is one of ultimate compassion in the face of extreme deprivation. Our family could take heart, believing in the basic goodness of people. But we also learned of cruelty and greed, light and dark, side by side. This was a haunting story that taught us grim wisdom at an early age. I would hazard a guess that many family legacy stories teach similar truths.

Telling

A family legacy story is one most family members have already heard—perhaps one that has been passed down for generations. It is important that you don't assume that every family member knows the structure of the story; they may have only retained a few details. As you fill in the blanks, you may find that one character becomes more important than another, depending on your audience. For example, your full appreciation of the story might change if you realize that every family member has a role in family legacy. Over time, your telling will vary along with your insights.

Your family legacy story has an essential structure. Once you've discovered the story's structure and its full narrative arc, reduce the sequence of events to a simple outline form. By doing so, you'll be able to tell the story without memorizing it and able to adapt it to different occasions.

Outline the story, stripping details down to keywords

and indicating its narrative arc.

For example, here is an outline of Shoemaker's Apprentice:

1. Setting: Streets of Munich, Germany, 1889, village of Tittling, Bavarian Forest

2. Characters: Grandfather, half-sister, godparents, stepparents, mother's relatives

3. First scene: Rising action, Ludwig begging for old leather, shoemaker's apprentice

4. Second scene: Rising action, Ludwig at the pastry shop, discovered by half-sister

5. Third scene: Rising action, return to the village, uproar at his illness, treatment

6. Resolution: Austrian Alps, monastery, immigrant to South Dakota, cowboy

7. Lesson: Compassion, resilience, stoicism, and survival

Using the outline as a base and keeping it in a digital or print file, adapt your legacy story to an audio or video file in order to preserve it.

Chapter Four offers other ways to work on the structure of the story, such as a story map, mind map, and storyboard. You'll also find important tips on how to tell the story effectively.

The "Seven Steps to Storytelling" were original to the Word Weaving Storytelling Project and featured throughout its highly successful, professional trainings for educators. These demystify the art of storytelling into easy-to-learn steps.

Exercises & Prompts: Family Legacy

Story Search

1. Recall a family story you've heard repeatedly taking place two to three generations back in time

2. Jot down the story or a fragment you remember

3. Identify its source: Who told you the story, and who told them?

4. Interview or consult other family members for their versions

5. Research and review family records, letters, archives, documents

6. Place the legacy story in a historical context

7. Consider the lessons of the story

8. Write down why this legacy story is important to the family identity

Ancestors: Their Stories

1. List all the ancestors that you can remember, going two to three generations back

2. Reflect on your favorite story about each of them, either told by them or others

3. Choose one and write that story in an outline

4. Write a paragraph about what you learned from this story, including some value, some strength you admire, or some understanding the story provides you about your ancestor and his or her life, times, and challenges

5. Repeat steps 1 to 4 with other ancestors

6. Look for a pattern in all the legacy stories you've gathered

7. Choose stories and patterns to benefit young generations

Storytellers Share Secrets: Family Legacy

Legacy stories have staying power. They tell of a challenge or situation that is central to the identity of a family, one that lasted over generations. Many of these tales are immigrant stories, since the United States is for the most part a country of immigrants. Those whose families were part of colonial times often have a long heritage of family legacy stories. Pioneer families as well as survivors of the Civil War and of slavery might have settlement stories. Native Americans enjoy an enduring tradition of storytelling, some of it sacred and mythic. Whatever the history of a given family, there are stories that were told, rumored, or passed along because their lessons were important to the family's identity or survival.

Creating

Bev Scott decided to use what she learned from her family legacy story as a foundation to write a historical novel, *Sarah's Secret: A Western Tale of Betrayal and Forgiveness.* In addition to her thirty-seven-year consulting career, Bev served as the executive director for a community action agency during the "War on Poverty," and taught sociology to undergraduates at both Cornell College and Coe College in Iowa and in the Organization Psychology master's program at John F. Kennedy University in the San Francisco Bay Area. She has written many professional articles and has published three books, the latest of which was coauthored with Kim Barnes, *Consulting on the Inside.*

Bev Scott

I longed to uncover the secrets of my grandfather's life after hearing rumors at a family reunion. My father had very little information about his father, and my grandmother refused to talk about him. All we knew was there was a thirty-year difference in their ages and that my grandfather had served in the Civil War. It seemed to me that the rumors must have some connection to the secrets my grandmother refused to share, and I vowed to uncover the story. When my career wound down, I finally had time to pursue it.

My aunt helped me find the dates of my grandfather's enlistment and service in the Union Army. I headed to the National Archives in Washington, DC, whose holdings document the lives of the men who served in the Civil War. I wanted to learn as much as I could about his life. The staff provided me with two unexpectedly thick folders of documents, forms, and correspondence. I had no idea the papers and documents in those files would not only reveal the secrets my grandmother had kept so long, but also provide the details of a fascinating story.

Based on dubious rumors heard about her grandfather at a family reunion, Bev became motivated to discover the truth. The legacy story that she uncovered using the dates of his Civil War military records was shocking, but vital to the family's identity. The fact that she was driven to conduct such an impressive research project indicated its significance. Family legacy stories are not always heroic tales, but they reflect the lives of our ancestors and their essential qualities—these are the stories that shaped the family. In Bev's search, as with many others who pursue legacy stories, there was no substitute for personally traveling to find primary documents in archives, in library newspaper files, or in a cemetery. In order to create a legacy story, Bev assembled the facts, records, and reports into a captivating narrative to tell.

Crafting

Grandfather's Deception

Bev Scott

A year after my grandfather, H.D. Scott, died in 1911, my grandmother, Ellen, had a visitor from the Pension Bureau to tell her the results of her request for widow's benefits. Ellen had been confident she would receive the benefits. As a veteran of the Civil War, H.D. had finally received his first pension check a month before he died. These benefits would support the family and help them build a house on the land claim she had filed outside Thedford, Nebraska. While they waited, she and her three younger children lived in a tent, while the older two boys worked on their uncle's farm.

The government agent described her situation: "She hopes to establish a home for herself and children; but it looks like a most hazardous undertaking as she is practically an invalid because of rheumatism [sic], and her children are undersized, puny-looking, little fellows, and they are more than a mile from the nearest water... In their present desolate surroundings, their condition is pitiable in the extreme."

Ellen had welcomed this visitor, anxious to hear the expected good news. Instead, the man informed her that she was not H.D.'s legal wife and therefore was not eligible to receive widow's benefits. H.D. had a prior family and had never divorced. The agent writes in his report: "...until I informed her of the fact, claimant declares she had no knowledge of the existence of a former wife. Her grief and tears were convincing of the truth. She begged me not to tell anyone in her home neighborhood."

Humiliated, Ellen shared no information about the deception of her husband with anyone. Despite her crippling rheumatoid arthritis, she pulled herself together and returned to work as a schoolteacher. She eventually became a school superintendent, all while raising her family.

Now I knew why no one in our family had heard about my grandfather—about his other legal wife and children.

Setting the stage for this extraordinary tale, Bev relates the bare facts of a government pension case, as well as the confident anticipation of a positive outcome. By quoting directly from the worker's comments, we see the dire conditions of Bev's grandmother's widowhood and of her young, pioneering family. The National Archives report adds substance and credibility to the narrative; his descriptive prose makes him part of the storytelling. This story summary has all the features of a legacy story, including a relevant historical context.

For Bev and her extended family, her grandmother was an inspiration: her life was a demonstration that we can overcome the setbacks we encounter in life through strength, resilience, and determination.

Creating

Waights Taylor Jr. was born and raised in Birmingham, Alabama, and has written five books, starting with two nonfiction books: *Alfons Mucha's Slav Epic: An Artist's History of the Slavic People* (2008), and the award-winning *Our Southern Home: Scottsboro to Montgomery to Birmingham—The Transformation of the South in the Twentieth Century* (2011). An award-winning murder mystery trilogy followed, featuring private detectives Joe McGrath and Sam Rucker: *Kiss of Salvation* (2014), *Touch of Redemption* (2016), and *Heed the Apocalypse* (2017).

Waights Taylor Jr.

How do you find the inspiration for family folklore in your memory bank? The obvious answers are simple: find stories passed down from generations, research archival material in today's digital age, and access personal memory and the memory of others. So what's the big deal? Consider this quote from the first sentence in chapter one of Jill Ker Conway's book, *When Memory Speaks: Exploring the Art of*

Autography: "Why is the autobiography the most popular form of fiction for modern readers?"

That rhetorical question is packed with meaning and controversy: meaning because Conway reminds us how suspect memory can be and controversy because the family folklore purist will say that, while memory can be suspect, it is a necessary liability in telling and retelling family stories that are considered true enough. I have written nonfiction and fiction, and all my books have used some elements of my family stories in the telling. To illustrate the successes and pitfalls I encountered in my nonfiction book, which was part memoir and mostly history, I will summarize one story.

Historian that he is, Waights Taylor Jr. discloses the controversial nature of published memoirs and their reputed twisting of facts. At the same time, he realizes that we are all unreliable witnesses to our personal experiences—that we bend the facts without consciously knowing we're doing so. This is often true in how we recall family members: we desire one legacy over another. In Waights' recollection of his Southern father during the presidential election of 1948, Waights cast his father as a hero for civil rights. Yet his childhood memory began to conflict with further information and was never resolved—until he read the newspaper files he found on a research visit to Livingston, Alabama.

Crafting

My Father, My Hero

Waights Taylor Jr.

My book, *Our Southern Home: Scottsboro to Montgomery to Birmingham—The Transformation of the South in the Twentieth Century*, tells mostly historical stories, but is also partly memoir. One personal story illustrates both the value and pitfalls of depending on memory alone to tell a family story.

In 1948, issues of racism and segregation fractured the Democratic Party Convention, causing the racist Dixiecrat Party led by Strom Thurmond to bolt from the Democratic Party. In 1949, my father was the editor of a small newspaper in Livingston, a small town in west-central Alabama. Dad wrote a number of editorials excoriating the Dixiecrat Party for leaving the Democratic Party and nominating Strom Thurman as their presidential candidate, thus threatening President Truman's reelection. Dad received little support for this point of view, and many labeled him a Communist. The local Ku Klux Klan threatened to burn a cross in our yard, and I was jeered at and teased by elementary school classmates. At that time, I was bursting with pride at my dad's principles.

As I grew older, Dad morphed into a right-wing bigot. *Who was this man?* I asked.

The answer finally appeared during my book tour in Alabama in 2012, when I was able to read other issues of Dad's newspaper from 1949; I found an editorial where Dad wrote, "we must protect our Southern way of life," a euphemism for segregation, even as he excoriated the Dixiecrats. So while Dad was a Southern liberal and a staunch supporter of FDR, his Southern liberalism did not extend to African Americans. As the years rolled by, the changes fostered by the Civil Rights Movement were more than Dad could comprehend or accept.

As Dad aged, he and I had many difficult arguments about politics which were not satisfactorily resolved. Yet when our arguments ran out of steam, we smiled at each other and always said, "I love you." Memory is a tenuous thing, and my youthful enthusiasm led me off the mark, but, in 1949, my father was my hero.

In this narrative, Waights brings us inside his thought process as he attempts to understand his father's legacy—both its positive and negative aspects. By posing the problem of faulty memory in sharing family stories, he makes that issue the main conflict and poses a larger question: how can we be certain a family legacy story is correct? As Waights continues to research the dichotomy of his father's stance on the Dixiecrat Party, opinions that angered the KKK, whose members made threats of burning a cross on the family lawn, he consults 1949 newspaper archives. Since his father wrote editorials for the paper, Waights could find actual documentation that his father's acceptance of Democratic Party policies was strictly economic and did not extend to the civil rights of African Americans.

Waights resolved the conflicts within his own memory by staying true to his boyhood beliefs of his father's heroic stance in 1948. No doubt this "mistaken" legacy was an inspiration to Waights and shaped his own willingness to take a further liberal stand in his adult life. Nevertheless, Waights learned the limits of his father's liberalism much later and tempered his understanding with reality. He ends the family legacy story with a final resolution: love and acceptance.

212 | Story Power

Do we put our thumb on the scale when we recall family legacy stories? Do we tilt them to the positive or negative side? It all depends on who's telling the story. But as both Bev and Waights discovered in their legacy stories, research makes all the difference. Today, there are many resources to verify the histories of ancestors. By doing so, we can reclaim a measure of truth and create a balanced family legacy of stories.

Patchwork Quilt

This chapter has explored the many facets of family stories: their various types and how they affect us. There is no doubt that family stories have a powerful influence on us, even when they are half forgotten or buried. **Family stories have a direct impact in how we perceive ourselves and our future.**

In this chapter, we've demonstrated how to gather family stories from a variety of sources: memories, relatives, photos, scrapbooks, archives, and cemeteries. Several contributors and I have shared secrets in how to select, create, and craft compelling family stories around the themes of Family Folklore, Secrets & Shadows, and Legacy. As you make the storytelling art your own, you'll experiment with our techniques and find your own methods or a combination.

The three themes modeled in this chapter are frequently selected for family stories, but they can overlap: a family secret can be a legacy story, for example. The chapter themes are presented in a way that shows the purpose of each one, as well as some of the difficulties in collecting and telling each type of family story. Research and primary source documents can be the arbiter of memory and buried secrets, but each story has its own truth.

Like a colorful, patchwork quilt, family stories bring us comfort: They give us a sense of belonging and create a core identity that can be a great source of empowerment. By sharing family stories, live and in person, we can affect change in our family dynamic. We gain strength by deepening our connections as we learn from one another and listen to the voices of many generations. We can face an unknown future of rapid change by hearing the transcendent lessons spoken by those who love us most, through their stories.

Chapter Four

Telling the Story: Techniques & Delivery

I'll tell you a secret. Old storytellers never die.
They disappear into their own story.

—Vera Nazarian, author

Introduction

The telling of stories is a tantalizing art—the magnetism of a good story is strong; it both pulls in the teller and draws in the audience. Even if you just share a hilarious tale worthy of a stand-up comic, you cross the threshold into a world of the imagination made of nothing but thin air. The very simplicity of the art is deceptive in its power to move an idea, create an experience, or produce a drama. A contributing factor is that members of the storytelling audience become co-creators in the art.

One extraordinary event demonstrated the stunning truth of that co-creation: I was to be the dinner entertainment for hundreds of teachers in a massive, all-purpose room in a public school, with a formal stage at one end and cafeteria tables scattered throughout. The clatter of the buffet service and the din of voices echoed in the brightly lit, institutional hall. I stood in front of a dusty, closed curtain on the edge of the stage, gripping a handheld microphone, preparing to tell the story of Scheherazade and her murderous husband, Sultan Schahriar. There was no spotlight—I stood in the shadows, waiting for a silence that never came. I was especially nervous because I'd invited a theater friend to observe my performance who was the Tony award-winning, artistic director of a Southern California repertory company.

As I began to tell the tale of Scheherazade, the first narrative of *A Thousand and One Nights*, the background noise in the hall lessened. Instinctively, I grew stock-still, with no hand gestures or body movement at all. Somehow, I knew that the more focused I was on voice production, the more the restless audience would listen. I felt like a statue, a disembodied live voice off to the side of the stage. With no cameras, no stage set, no lighting, and no supporting cast, I abandoned my dramatic style. My tall theater friend, Marty, was standing along the sidelines watching. Afterwards, over drinks, he commented on the storytelling performance as a tribute to the human imagination: both mine and that of the audience. **That bare, naked, stripped-down presentation highlighted the essential dynamic of the art, a shared production of story by both teller and listeners.**

Telling a story is like painting a picture with words. Storytelling is an amazingly inexpensive art. There is really nothing else needed besides the live human voice, listeners, and a clear story focus. Your inner concentration on the images embedded in a story drives your voice production to create the word pictures that every listener sees in his or her own way. It's a triangulation of creativity among teller, story, and listener that resonates and continues to develop throughout the telling.

But how do you create an inner concentration strong enough to maintain focus in a challenging setting? **How does the teller create the images that everyone can see?** The following steps are designed to assist you in doing just that.

Seven Steps to Storytelling

Guidebooks promise to take you from here to there: to becoming an accomplished expert in a field. I want to take you along some well-trodden steps, the pathway of minstrels, troubadours, and shamans—and sometimes of con men. Many practice the art of illusion, but authentic, personal stories have the undeniable power to connect.

These seven steps are proven to work: they have demystified the storytelling art for many thousands trained in the Word Weaving Storytelling Project. These steps concentrate on the internal elements of the framing process, and they do not reduce the art to a superficial set of delivery skills. Taken one by one, each step adds to the depth of the storytelling experience so that it is an unforgettable one.

Seven Steps: The Basic Technique[1]

1. Select a story you want to tell.

2. Learn the structure and frame the story in sections.

3. Visualize the settings and characters.

4. See the action take place as if you're watching a silent movie.

5. Tell the story aloud, using your voice to project the images you've visualized.

---

1 Farrell, Catharine. *Storytelling: A Guide for Teachers.* New York: Scholastic Professional Books, 1991.

6. Learn the story by heart, not word-for-word (*layers of meaning*).

7. Practice telling the story until it comes naturally.

1. Story Selection: Throughout the first three chapters, we've discussed and modeled many ways to find, select, and create a story worth telling. Using examples of popular story themes from a diverse group of contributors, we've shared a variety of tips for story selection. Some storytellers follow their emotional charge in recalling an experience; some use an object, a photo, a prompt, a journal, or a writing exercise. All of these are compelling ways to begin this first step of story selection.

Whatever process you use, the story that begins to come into focus must eventually have these essential features for a personal narrative to be effective and memorable:

- Setting
- Characters
- Conflict, tension
- Narrative arc of rising action, increasing tension
- Sensory images within the action
- Dialogue within the action, if possible
- Resolution of conflict

Continue to refine your memory of an incident to improve recall of sensory details and the inherent conflict or problem. The conflict or rising action can be an expectation or the anticipatory beginning of an adventure—whatever makes us sit up, listen, and ask that all-important question: What happens next? **It could be a high-stakes or low-stakes scenario, as long as the outcome is uncertain.**

In addition to a narrative arc with rising and falling action, consider the setting, sensory details, characters, and dialogue. Just one or two lines of dialogue can bring a personal story to life.

2. **Frame the story in sections.** Once you've selected a story, frame it using keywords and images, if possible. Draw the structure of the story any way you wish: with a storyboard to show the scenes, an outline to lists its sequence, a narrative arc to show the rise and fall of action, perhaps on index cards with a section of the tale on each card, or with a mind map. Whatever form you use, you are now determining the shape of the story.

Be aware that this is not a script, but a framing with trigger words, drawings, and images. A written script tends to restrict a spontaneous telling that is interactive with the audience. Often, these graphic organizers are all you need to tell an effective story and to keep a record of your repertoire.

See the graphic organizers in this chapter for some tools in creating the structure of your story.

3. **Visualize the Settings and Characters.** Put the graphic organizer or index cards aside and close your eyes. Imagine each setting as if it were a movie set. Forget the plot for a moment and look around your story's environment. Notice small details; see color and light. You are invisible on the set. All your senses function except your hearing. For now, the imaginary world of your story is silent.

This exercise calls upon your powers of concentration and may produce sketchy results at first. But stay with it. If you can see only a few sensory details, try to sustain them for as long as you are able. With practice, you'll be able to use your intention to step into the atmosphere after a rainstorm for example: feel the slippery, wet grass, smell the distant rain, feel the damp chill on your skin, pick the battered rose in the garden, or taste the tangy bite of a fallen apple.

Now that you have a good mental picture of the setting, add the characters and their habits. See their mouths move as they talk and make facial expressions and hand gestures. Notice their clothes, their coloring, the expression in their eyes, and how they move. With this step, you have built and populated the world of the story with your accurate memory and focused imagination.

Not yet allowing yourself to hear anything does temporarily hold your creativity in check. It is an artificial device, one I learned from my storytelling teacher, Mae Durham Roger, who learned it from the famous storyteller, Ruth Sawyer, in her iconic book *The Way of the Storyteller*. Decades before Ruth Sawyer, Marie Shedlock considered storytelling a "miniature play" with the "inward eye" as the "stage," as she wrote in her 1915 book, *The Art of the Story-Teller*.

After completing this exercise, you might want to revise your notes or add details to your graphic organizer.

4. See the action take place as if you're watching a silent movie. Close your eyes and run the silent movie of the full story. Begin with the first segment of your story and let the action roll. If you can't visualize the story from beginning to end, keep trying: go back to your graphic organizer and start again. As you watch the story scenes move in exact sequence, get a sense for which are fast-paced and which move slowly. Let the story build to its climactic scene, then let it wind down to the end. Switch off your silent movie projector.

This is the most important part of storytelling preparation. To the extent that you can visualize the story clearly in your mind's eye, pausing within its structure, you'll be able to speed it up, slow it down, adapt it to different listeners or audiences, and change it each time you tell it. When I practice for a storytelling presentation, I often have my eyes closed, reviewing the action, setting, and characters. This is a much more essential step than rehearsing a written script.

5. Tell the story aloud, using your voice to project the images you've visualized. Using your voice is the most exciting and magical step of all. The reason you've been a silent witness to the story settings, characters, and action is to keep your creative, inner focus on the visual and sensory elements. You create all the sound the story will ever have. Your voice is the story's soundtrack: You provide a credible description, narrative, dialogue, sound effects, and emotional tone.

Switch on the silent movie of your story, saying the words aloud as you watch the action unfold. Use your voice to literally produce the images—in thin air. Imagine a movie screen hovering like a holograph in the middle of the room and fill it with the story images you see in your mind's eye. Listen to your own words change as you describe new details or hear new dialogue. You might pause as you search for new words to match your inner vision and to achieve fluency.

Refer to your graphic organizer as a cue if you're stuck, and then start over. Tell your story a few times, refining the expression of your voice to reflect the story's images, emotions, and dialogue. You might record your telling of the story and listen to your own voice as you continue to build the inner world with the eye of your imagination. Seeing and telling is a dynamic, powerful practice.

6. Learn the story by heart, not word-for-word (*layers of meaning*). Deepen your connection to the story by isolating the truth in the story and relating it to your own truths. Spend time doing some research to verify the accuracy of your personal story. Consult with friends or family members who were there or had similar experiences. Even though you might not add the details you discover through research or learn from eyewitnesses to the tale, they verify what you have remembered. You might then listen to your recording of the story and close your eyes, at a time when you are most relaxed. Think about what the symbolism of the story means to you. Your understanding of the layers of meaning in a story greatly adds to the telling of it. This is the subtext: it tells what cannot be said.

7. Practice telling the story until it comes naturally. There are any number of ways to practice telling a story. You could play your own recorded story and join in with your live voice until there is no hesitation in the flow of words. Recruit your family, friends, or pets for a live audience—that is often the best way. Tell it to a mirror without notes and watch your facial expressions and hand gestures. Videotape your telling and play it back. For further refinement and to embed the story deeply within your mind, tell it while you're driving, jogging, or showering.

A story when told is never perfectly performed because it is always changing. Storytelling is an interactive, dynamic art whose listeners are co-creators. Spontaneity modifies and adapts the telling to each new audience and situation.

Delivery Techniques

Spoken delivery in the art of storytelling can take many forms, among them: conversational or social sharing, a professional exchange, or a performance. Once a story is prepared to tell in many formats or venues, it becomes a powerful tool that can enhance and empower your communication skills.

Conversational storytelling: Telling a story in a social setting is the most lively and interactive way to share a personal story—listeners can interject, respond, and comment. Using narratives told in the flow of the moment, some conversationalists capture the attention of a group without effort, easily launching into well-crafted tales. Others repeat the same old stories and often bore their friends and family, even when the tales are told with animation and humor. What makes an informal story unforgettable in this milieu? Is the memorable story one that is convincing or that creates a bridge to a deeper understanding?

First, choose a story that is relevant to the topic at hand, one that extends or enriches the exchange. Look for a hook to bring immediate notice, or else use a transition as you begin. For example, if the conversation revolves around high school memories, you might startle your audience by saying, "When I was in eighth grade, I wanted to go into a convent instead of high school." Once you've grabbed their attention, begin with a scene. Use sensory details to set the action, use a bit of dialogue, and continue with the tension or conflict.

> Just before graduation, I decided to visit my school
> principal's office alone and let Sister Bernard know how
> serious I was about becoming a convent postulant and
> taking vows of poverty, chastity, and obedience. "Are you
> sure?" she asked, frowning. "Do your parents know?" I
> convinced her of both, and she gave me a list of what to
> bring to the convent: how many socks, underwear, and pairs
> of shoes. I would wear the habit of a postulant, a black robe
> with a cap and a veil down the back. "You would not have to
> shave off your hair," she said.

As you tell your story, call up the images of each scene in
your mind's eye. Project them on an imaginary small screen
somewhere in midair. This is the key technique to having
the story connect: as you visualize the events and project the
scenes, your listeners will also see them and experience the
action vicariously. You might literally "lean in" over a table
or countertop to increase the intimacy and speak directly to
each person in turn. Be aware of the rising action and keep
the thread of your story going throughout the interactive
nature of conversing. Return to the narrative and resolve the
tension: What happens? What do you learn during the story's
events? How does the story relate to the overall discussion?
Conversational storytelling can be a practice session for telling
the same story in a more challenging venue.

Professional storytelling: This is a more formal setting that
has fewer distractions during its telling than a social story. A
professional story advances your career or makes a point about
your expertise and could take place in an interview, a public
talk, or a classroom setting. In this presentation, it is important
to be well prepared so that you are able to touch on the major
points before or after your story. Consider the story types in
Chapter Two and prepare one that matches the requirements

of your position or purpose: a defining story, signature story, or a personal brand. Create the layers of meaning for this story so you ready to answer questions or expand on it further in a talk. What does this story demonstrate about you or about the topic?

While delivering this story, employ the subtext of confidence so that you communicate your credibility along with the narrative. Practice eye contact to include everyone in a natural, random way. Visualize each scene and project its reality with the steady quality of your voice. Keep your focus on the point of the story, rather than on its drama. While there must be rising action to maintain the interest of your audience, the purpose of the narrative is not primarily to entertain. It is to market, to promote, to demonstrate, or to persuade. Use a minimum of hand gestures or body language, and avoid pacing. This is the time to stand in your truth.

Performance: And now, lights, camera, and action! This is the spectacular traditional art of storytelling to a live audience of any age. However, the nature of its drama differs from that of a play in that there is no fourth wall as there is in a theatrical performance. The teller speaks to and includes the audience in an interactive process of story-making. Further, the story does not take place on the stage, and the spotlight is not on the storyteller. The arena for the story is the entire theater, hall, or room. It takes place within the imaginations both of the teller and of all those listening.

So, claim the space! Imagine a line around and above the listeners: this is the story's sphere—this is where it happens. It could be called the *story tent* for a one-ring circus. **It is this story tent made of thin air that is *your* canvas—where you paint pictures with your spoken words**. In the telling, your images merge with those of your listeners in an open-ended, accessible, invisible, holographic display.

As you tell the story, you possess a double vision: the inner eye that focuses on the setting, characters, and action of the tale, and the outer eye that seeks to connect with every listener. This bifocal ability is different from that of the actor who concentrates on an inner interpretation of his character. He does not directly engage the audience nor does he conjure up the specifics of setting, props, or other characters. The storyteller is a one-act player—the teller embodies the entirety of the story drama, while at the same time eagerly connecting with those listening. Even if the group is too large to see everyone, the teller appears to make eye contact by looking at various sections of the room in a continuous sweep.

Vocalization is important: the rise and fall of volume, the use of different voices in dialogue, the clear articulation of words. A voice coach can be an enormous help in learning how to speak from the diaphragm, and not strain your vocal cords. Practicing and recording your own voice is an excellent way to hear the sound of your voice, your skill in dialogue, and your pacing. While learning fluency in storytelling, become aware of the importance of the pause. Your audience needs a break in the flow of words to absorb them, to internalize their meaning, and to create their own visuals. The musical score of your storytelling drama is the emotional tone of your voice and your subtext—what isn't said. Listen for the emotional tone and how it changes.

Since the greatest focus during delivery is voice production of the story in all its aspects, there is little need for large hand gestures, actual props, or

costumes. That is the simplicity of the art. Some professional performers do wear costumes and might have musical accompaniment, but these only enhance the art; they are not necessary elements. Some theatrical storytellers "act out" the characters in the story more completely by moving to different parts of the stage to speak in character, then as narrator, then as another character. These techniques might add to the storytelling experience, but also might distract. Be alert to the possibility of a dramatic telling that shifts away from the shared, co-creative experience of the audience.

It is the identification of the audience with the story that makes it unforgettable. Only when the audience experiences the story as their own do they remember it as if they lived it. This is the power in the art of storytelling.

Media Options

Today, in our high-tech world, there are numerous ways to tell a story. All of them can engage listeners with some interaction.

A written story is told through articles, blog posts, or even on social media, such as a Twitter thread. Short, personal brand stories can be highlighted on a website or in promotional print materials.

A spoken story can be told in person, in a social setting, as a performance, or for a professional presentation, pitch, or panel. TED talks are considered spoken stories. The Moth story competitions or story slams are popular and feature episodes around themes. **Because of their live, unedited nature, spoken stories require more practice and skill to convey images and elicit emotions in others.** This is by far the most effective option.

An audio story is spoken aloud but recorded. Audio stories are usually in podcast form. With today's technology, creating an audio story is more possible than ever—then it can be distributed on social media or through a subscription. Storytelling podcasts are currently part of public radio programming and can be enjoyed either live or streamed from the archives of the broadcasts.

A digital story is told through a variety of visual media, such as video, animation, interactive formats such as Wattpad, and even games. A YouTube channel is an inexpensive way to launch a storytelling platform since the video quality is not as important as conveying the powerful experience of a given story.

Tools & Organizers

Each graphic is merely a suggestion or for use as a starter concept. Adapt them to your own use, or create new ones.

Story Board

Mind Web - Story Map 1

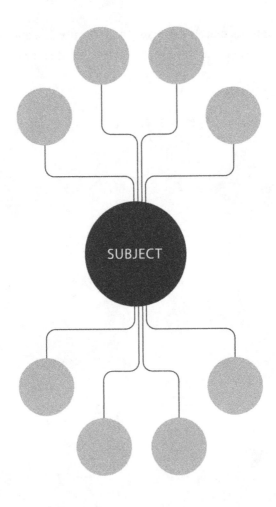

Story Map 2 - Outline template

SETTING:

WHERE:

WHEN:

▼

MAJOR CHARACTERS:

MAJOR CHARACTERS:

▼

PLOT/PROBLEM:

▼   ▼   ▼

| EVENT 1: | EVENT 3: | EVENT 3: |

▼

OUTCOME:

Chapter Five

The Heritage of Folklore

"Stories lean on stories, cultures on cultures."

—Jane Yolen, fantasy and children's author

Introduction

"Once upon a time"—that magical phrase conjures up fantastical realms that exist outside of time, in the forever after. Such is the nature of the ancient craft of traditional storytelling, of timeless, wondrous narratives with symbolic patterns and supernatural events, stories told by no one and everyone. It is the fabulous world of folklore, a spontaneous, oral body of literature that has no authors and no boundaries nor era, passed down by word of mouth for millennia. Within these captivating tales are talking animals, magical waters, fairy godmothers, enchanted castles deep in a forest, and flying carpets.

But as our global community shrinks to the size of a village, our stories not only lean on one another, they merge and change. The ever-evolving art of storytelling is adapting to our postmodern era of rapid progress. What was once considered the ultimate method of transmitting the values of a culture—its traditional tales—is now called into question.

With today's current emphasis on the individual and on truths that are directly experienced, there is a creative shift in the art away from traditional storytelling and its folklore to spontaneous, personal tales.

There are several reasons for this shift. All of them contribute to a new oral tradition or, as the prologue of Chris Anderson's book (*TED Talks: The Official TED Guide to Public Speaking*) states, "there is a new superpower that anyone, young or old, can benefit from. It's called *presentation literacy.*" Anderson imagines a new campfire and personal ways to convey truth based on direct experience that are available to everyone. It is a tremendously exciting time to practice the art of storytelling.

And so, in current society, the relevance of traditional tales is becoming problematic. Though some ancient tales continue to meet our storytelling needs, many of them do not. These stories are often told in a cultural context that is alien or that no longer connects to our common experience. In fact, in order for some folk and fairy tales to have any meaning at all, they require an extensive introduction to their listeners. For example, even "Jack and the Beanstalk" assumes some prior knowledge of dairy farming, cows, beans, and gardening. It can also be terrifying when children hear the giant's deep throated, singsong rhyme:

> Fee-fi-fo-fum
>
> I smell the blood of an Englishman.
>
> Be he alive or be he dead
>
> I'll grind his bones to make my bread.

Jack's thievery and malice can give rise to ethical questions: Should Jack have stolen the golden harp? Did he have to kill the giant? Somehow Jack's courage and initiative is lost in our modern quandaries. We might attempt an updated version, but sanitizing folktales is a tricky proposition, while fractured fairy tales do not make sense without knowing the original, sometimes brutal, version. There are countless examples of a folktale's setting that is so extremely unfamiliar that without copious contextual clues, the story itself can be meaningless or offensive.

Further, it is impossible to ignore male dominance in most centuries-old, traditional tales. Sexism abounds in the stories of princesses who need saving, stories whose protagonists are exclusively male. Most women in folktales play a passive role, while women with any power tend to be secondary characters like wicked stepmothers or fairy godmothers. Feminist collections of fairy tales that feature girls and women as independent-minded maidens or princesses nevertheless exist within a patriarchal authoritarian context.

Recent studies show that though women make up nearly 50 percent of the world's population, there are not as many folktales about women. In a quantitative study led by Jonathan Gottschall in his book, *Literature, Science, and a New Humanities*, "it was found that this phenomenon is prevalent worldwide; that male main characters...outnumbered female main characters by more than two to one."

And Gottschall's count is itself misleading: Even in folktales in which the main character is female, the woman is often powerless and must be rescued, discovered, awoken, or kissed by a heroic male character. Obviously, it is impossible to retell the ancient, traditional tales: that bell has already been rung. Female storytellers can begin a new tradition for our time—speaking their own truth as heroines of their own personal stories.

Cultural appropriation is also an issue to consider when telling traditional multicultural folktales. This refers to a particular dynamic in which members of a dominant culture take elements from a culture of people who have been systematically oppressed by that dominant group. When we tell folktales from someone else's culture without permission, we can be appropriating, especially if we identify as a member of a dominant culture and tell folktales from minority groups. It is a sensitive and controversial issue, and one not to be ignored.

Nowadays, each teller continues to choose what folktales, myths, and legends to include in his or her repertoire, but with some caution and respectful mention. Still, the overriding principles to consider in story selection are: how relevant is the story to its contemporary audience, and how comfortable is the teller with embodying a tale from another culture? Since storytelling is an intimate, spoken art, each tale becomes personal—as if you lived it. Each storyteller must determine his or her own authenticity in "borrowing" from another culture's traditional lore.

Yet the very timelessness of the oral tradition ensures a continuity of stories, from those tales first uttered to those now told in our new age style. The stories we personally create may not have princesses, magic, or dragons, but the basic story elements remain the same. Perhaps our collective minds can only interpret experience in a finite number of ways. Both folktales told throughout the ages and the contemporary ones we now tell one another seem to fall within certain patterns.

It would be good to see where your personal stories fit: What motifs are you repeating, what tale types do you tell, and what archetypes do you choose?

Folktale Motifs

A *motif* is the smallest element of a folktale that persists in the oral tradition. **Folktale motifs are recurring thematic elements found in tales throughout disparate cultures.** Examples of common motifs include journeys through dark forests, enchanted transformations, magical cures or other spells, encounters with helpful animals or mysterious creatures, foolish bargains, impossible tasks, clever deceptions, and many more. Some memorable and oft-repeated images are a lost shoe, a rapidly growing stalk, a spinning wheel, a poisoned fruit, a magic lamp. Motifs are the building blocks within the plot-patterns of folk and fairy tales, myths, and legends.

In the eighteenth and nineteenth centuries, folk and fairy tales were collected and published in numerous countries. These tales did not have "authors"— the Grimm brothers, Charles Perrault, and other collectors did not *write* the folktales, they merely transcribed story versions of narratives dictated to them by the common people, tales orally passed down for centuries. To study the tales, folklorists devised systems for cross-cultural and international reference. Folklorists analyzed, interpreted, and described the traditional elements found in the folklore of particular groups and compared the folklore of various regions and cultures of the world based on **motif patterns**.

The most well-known folktale classification systems are Aarne and Thompson's *The Types of the Folktale* (originally published by Antti Aarne in 1910, then revised in 1928 and 1961 by Stith Thompson, and in 2004 by Uther), and Thompson's *Motif Index of Folk-Literature* (originally published 1922–1936; second edition 1955–1958).

Folklorists found that similar folktale motifs are repeated in oral traditions of cultures all over the world—even in far-flung regions with no connection or contact with one another. No one really knows how this phenomenon occurs, but there are many theories. There seem to be universal patterns and images that repeat in folktales as a spontaneous, human expression. In the *Journal of Folklore Research*, Robert A. Georges states in his article, "The Centrality in Folkloristics of Motif and Tale Type":

> "...the constructs on which [the indexes] are based are derived from and mirror the ways that human beings conceptualize the stories they tell each other."

For example, Cinderella is one of the most told stories in the world—variants of the story appear in the folklore of many cultures. Folklorists disagree about how many versions of the tale exist, with estimates ranging from 350 to over 1,500, and it has its own Aarne-Thompson-Uther classification code, ATU 510A. One of the best candidates for the earliest Cinderella story is the Egyptian tale of Rhodopis.

The Rhodopis tale was first recorded by the Greek historian Strabo in the first century CE. It is considered to be loosely based on a real person—a Greek slave girl abducted and taken to Egypt—and a version of it was written down by Herodotus five hundred years before Strabo. The story of Yeh-hsien, also known as Yeh-Shen and Sheh Hsien, is the oldest known Cinderella tale recorded in China. It appears in *Yu Yang Tsa Tsu* (*Miscellany of Forgotten Lore*), which was written by Tuan Ch'êng-shih around the ninth century CE, although the tale was known centuries before.

The motifs in these two ancient tales are repeated in our familiar Cinderella fairy tale, but these stories of yesteryear were told by peoples of widely divergent cultures. The repeated motifs include: a kind, persecuted maid; a wicked stepmother; a magical helper; a fancy celebration; a lost garment, usually a shoe; and a secret identity revealed to a prince or man of wealth. If we strip these many Cinderella versions down to their core motif, it could be the *recognition of the ideal feminine identity*: The prince recognizes the maid for who she is—a lovely woman in rags—and realizes she is the woman he loves.

No doubt, the study of worldwide patterns of collected folk and fairy tales is fascinating. But are these patterns and motifs, still truly in use? Do we still tell the same stories in new cloth?

Exercises & Prompts: Motifs

Prompts: Motifs

1. What is your favorite fairy tale?

2. Close your eyes and recall its most vivid images.

3. What are your favorite folktale motifs?

4. What images do you remember the most?

5. Which images are the most charged?

6. Make a list of all the folk and fairy-tale images you recall on a notepad.

7. Match these images with your personal narratives.

Exercise

1. Can you identify motifs in your personal stories?

2. What images, situations, or characters do you repeat?

3. Make a list of any patterns you recognize.

Exercise

1. Make a list of the most memorable images or motifs from your favorite folktales or myths.

2. Create an original story with them.

3. Weave these images or motifs into a personal story.

Tale Types

The study of folktale motifs reveals the vivid imagery that creates persistent, indivisible, and defining narrative elements or story details. These motifs are the building blocks for common tale types. **Tale types are recurring, self-sufficient plots or motif groupings.** There are millions of folktales in the world, but many tales are variations on a limited number of themes. A tale type remains consistent, while its motifs may change as they adapt to a specific culture. The classification system originally designed by Aarne, and later revised first by Thompson, and later by Uther, is intended to bring out the similarities between tales by grouping variants of the same tale under the same ATU category.

According to the Aarne-Thompson-Uther (ATU) Classification of Folk Tales, now accessible online, there are seven tale type categories:

ATU Tale Type Index

1–299. Animal Tales

300–749. Tales of Magic

750–849. Religious Tales

850–999. Realistic Tales

1000–1199. Tales of the Stupid Ogre (or Giant, or Devil)

1200–1999. Anecdotes and Jokes

2000–2399. Formula Tales

Clicking on these various categories and subcategories online might stimulate your creative imagination during the creation of a personal story. Even simply referring to a tale type within your true story and using the tale type as an analogy might give added dimension to your own experiences. For example, the folktale type that captured my imagination as a child was "The Enchanted Pig" from Andrew Lang's *Red Fairy Book* (ATU 425). Though this tale type is described as a "quest for the vanished husband," I saw it as the **heroine's journey.** The wife needed to wear out three pairs of iron shoes, blunt a steel staff, and accomplish impossible tasks, while pregnant and giving birth along the way.

Looking back, did I know that being a single mother would be equally challenging? Was I preparing for the ordeal of self-sufficiency and motherhood? Or was this story a universal theme, telling of the impossible tasks that women face and must overcome? In the many versions of this tale type, the wife must rescue an animal/husband and restore him to human form. To me, that sounds like a modern story. I could easily incorporate a version of this tale type into real-life incidents I experienced as a single mother, doing the impossible—wearing out my iron shoes.

A more recent analysis of plot or tale types is the encyclopedic work of Christopher Booker, *The Seven Basic Plots: Why We Tell Stories.* In the introduction, Booker states:

> There are indeed a small number of plots which are so fundamental to the way we tell stories that it is virtually impossible for any storyteller ever entirely to break away from them... Once we become acquainted with [stories'] symbolic language and begin to catch something of its extraordinary significance, there is literally no story in the

world which cannot then be seen in a new light: because we have come to the heart of what stories are about and why we tell them.

Christopher Booker reflects on the deeper nature of storytelling and mythmaking through a decades-long analysis, one which was influenced by Carl Jung. Though Booker lists seven basic plots in the title of his book, he actually includes nine in the book itself, stating that the last two are more recent:

1. **Overcoming the Monster**: in which the hero must venture to the lair of a monster which is threatening the community, destroy it, and escape (often with a treasure).

2. **Rags to Riches:** in which someone who seems quite commonplace or downtrodden but has the potential for greatness manages to fulfill that potential.

3. **The Quest**: in which the hero embarks on a journey to obtain a great prize that is located far away.

4. **Voyage and Return:** in which the hero journeys to a strange world that at first is enchanting and then so threatening the hero finds he must escape and return home to safety.

5. **Comedy**: in which a community divided by frustration, selfishness, bitterness, confusion, lack of self-knowledge, lies, and so on must be reunited in love and harmony (often symbolized by marriage).

6. **Tragedy:** in which a character falls from prosperity to destruction because of a fatal mistake.

7. **Rebirth:** in which a dark power or villain traps the hero in a living death until he or she is freed by another character's loving act.

8. **Rebellion Against "The One":** in which the hero rebels against the all-powerful entity that controls the world until he is forced to surrender to that power.

9. **Mystery:** In which an outsider to some horrendous event (such as a murder) tries to discover the truth of what happened.

It's tempting to critique an overarching analysis such as this mammoth effort: the reduction of almost the entirety of world literature into seven or nine plot types. But Booker's system has value simply in how he is thinking about story: that there are basic story themes we all seem to use and that these have sustaining and compelling power. Storytellers can classify their own material in general categories as a way to reflect or define their purpose in sharing stories. For example, if you seek to entertain as a storyteller, you might not tell stories of rebirth. On the other hand, if you are a storyteller/facilitator in a penitentiary program, stories of rebellion and rebirth might be excellent tale types. Knowing that stories' basic themes are limited and that story material will repeat ancient patterns, whether those in folklore or literature, gives modern storytellers a shape and structure to their craft.

Exercises & Prompts: Tale Types

Prompts: Tale Types

1. What is your favorite plot type?

2. Close your eyes and recall its emotional effect.

3. What is your favorite fairy tale?

4. Why do you like it?

5. Which books do you read the most? What genre?

6. What plot types do most of your personal stories have?

7. What effect do you want your stories to have on your audience?

Exercise: Tale Types

1. Create a personal story based on one of the tale types in the Aarne-Thompson-Uther Index.

2. Write a personal story based on one of Booker's plot types.

3. Create a quest story in which the hero is a heroine or a nonbinary protagonist.

4. Write a story from personal experience that is a classic comedy.

5. Write another story from personal experience that is a classic tragedy.

Archetypes

The deepest layer of a story is the archetype: It arises
from the collective unconscious, a way of knowing that is
universal and symbolic. According to the psychologist Carl
Jung, archetypes are similar to dream images—folktales
with archetypes are a culture's way of dreaming out loud.
These symbolic images and situations are a type of coded,
imagistic language, messages from one level of consciousness
to another—from dreaming to our waking state. Though
archetypes exist in all art forms, the narrative form of story
transmits a powerful archetypal connection.

Folktales—by their very nature—express universal symbols
through an ancient cultural lens; they are the narrative type
most likely to contain archetypes. Fairy tales and myths, in
particular, access the realm of dreams, the chaotic fantasy
images of the unconscious. And just as it is difficult to interpret
dream imagery precisely, so it is challenging to define the
meaning of a given archetype. *We cannot know an archetype
from a description of its parts, but only in the context of
its story, when the full construct of its deeper meaning is
revealed.* Then we can relate; we know it without knowing it—
no standard plot analysis applies.

Understanding archetypes is like breathing underwater—it's a
hit-and-miss project, unsustainable. Yet we sense their impact
in how we react to their oblique meanings and how we repeat
their amorphous patterns in our own stories. When we use
archetypes in our personal stories, we can create a deeper,
lasting dimension—even if we do not fully appreciate their
multifaceted qualities.

As Carl Jung famously wrote:

> Not for a moment dare we succumb to the illusion that an archetype can be finally explained and disposed of. Even the best attempts at explanation are only more or less successful translations into another metaphorical language. (Indeed, language itself is only an image.) **The most we can do is *dream the myth onwards* and give it a modern dress.**

With that disclaimer, Jung described some notable archetypes throughout his voluminous works: **archetypal events** such as birth, death, separation from parents, initiation, task, quest, marriage, and the union of opposites; **archetypal figures** including the great mother, father, child, maiden, wise old man or woman, trickster, shadow, and hero or heroine; and **archetypal mythic motifs** like apocalypse, natural disaster, and creation.

In fairy tales and myths, we can often find a constellation of archetypes in a single story. For example, in the tale **Rumpelstiltskin** (ATU Motif Index 500: The Name of the Supernatural Helper), we see a number of archetypes at play: The **innocent maiden** must perform an **impossible task** necessitated by the greed of her father and her king/husband. Her situation is made worse by a **nameless trickster** who barters for her firstborn babe. As she **wanders into the woods**, she overhears his name, conquers him on her **third** guess, destroys the trickster, and keeps her child.

The meaning of this remarkable fairy tale, collected by the brothers Grimm in the nineteenth century, but with roots that go back four thousand years to the Bronze Age, is different for everyone who hears it. It all depends on how the multilayered symbology resonates with the listener. Stories like this one tell what cannot be said. As John Murray, a British literary commentator, wrote recently in an online blog, "Many mysteries about 'Rumpelstiltskin' remain, defying analysis or explication. In summary, it's a fairy tale whose central character has no clear motive, and a story which withholds its own meaning from us. It just exists…"

That's the dilemma of archetypes: they make sense on a symbolic, emotional level and nonsense on an intellectual level. However, I do understand the meaning of Rumpelstiltskin. My personal, "modern dress" take on this fairy tale is: a young maid is a pawn to patriarchal society and its greed until she "names" the trickster, and in so doing, *knows* how to perform the impossible task and is empowered—she spins her own gold and keeps her own child. **The "innocent maiden" and the "wily trickster" are opposites of the same character who then integrate into one, as is often the case with character archetypes**. But it's very possible that we as a culture have distanced ourselves from the ancient way of recognizing archetypes at a primal level. In our postmodern era, perhaps we need to create new narratives beyond the patriarchal and agricultural symbologies—and spin a modern dress.

Exercises & Prompts: Archetypes

Prompts: Archetypes

1. Reflect on your personal stories: who is your character archetype?

2. What archetypal character from a fairy tale or myth could you incorporate into a story?

3. What settings in nature have a deep meaning for you?

4. What tasks or conflicts have universal meaning for many?

5. Do you find any parallels between a personal story and a fairy tale or myth?

6. What is your shadow archetype?

Exercise: Archetypes

1. Keep a dream journal and use your entries as a resource for personal stories.

2. Write a story based on a dream, or add dream images to a true story.

3. Write down a list of your most frequent dream images: good, bad, and ugly.

4. Explore the meaning of your dream images.

5. Notice parallels in your personal stories.

Exercise: Archetypes

1. What are the archetypes in your favorite fairy tales?

2. List your own character archetypes in various stories.

3. List your animal archetypes.

4. List the settings that are archetypes for you.

5. Name your situational archetypes: the events that are pivotal.

6. Write a story with some of these archetypes.

7. Tell it out loud, record it, and listen to it.

By making artistic use of motifs, tale types, and story archetypes, modern storytellers can create a new tradition of storytelling—a new age of fire. Our global village needs stories that speak directly to us, now more than ever.

As Mark Turner, cognitive scientist, linguist, and author of *The Literary Mind: The Origins of Thought and Language* states, in looking to the future:

> Narrative imagining—story—is the fundamental instrument of thought. Rational capacities depend upon it. It is our chief means of looking into the future, or predicting, or planning, and of explaining.

Meet
the Contributors

Lisa Alpine is the author of *Wild Life: Travel Adventures of a Worldly Woman* (Foreword Reviews' Gold Medal Book of the Year Award) and *Exotic Life: Travel Tales of an Adventurous Woman* (first place, North American Book Awards). Her story "Fish Trader Ray" received the Silver Solas Medal for Best Travel Story of the Year. Other awards include: Solas Gold 2019 Best Travel Memoir for "Ole in Paris"; Bronze Best Humor 2019 for "The Twerking Nun of Korce"; Honorable Mention 2019 for "Where God, Anchovies, and Flamenco Reside"; and Best Women's Travel for "Sugar Granny and Her Dancing Shoes." Alpine is currently scribing stories for her next book, *Dance Life: Movin' and Groovin' Around the Globe*. Albanian salsa stories will grace its pages as well as her dance and travel experiences in Cuba, Mexico, the Republic of Georgia, Armenia, Paris, Spain, and other exotic locales. When not wrestling with words, exploring the ecstatic realms of dance, swimming with sea creatures, or waiting for a flight, Alpine is tending her orchards in Northern California and the Big Island of Hawai'i. Read her monthly online magazine about travel, dance, writing, health, and inspiration at www.lisaalpine.com.
Chapter One: Adventure Stories

Lisa Bishop, MLIS, is a graduate of the School of Library and Information Science, San Jose State University—part of a groundbreaking group of teachers reinvigorating the San Francisco Unified School District (SFUSD) school library program. Prior to her graduate degree, she became certified as a BCLAD Spanish bilingual teacher and national board-certified teacher. She was the International Baccalaureate coordinator at Flynn Elementary School, working toward it becoming the first public PYP IB school in SFUSD. She created the "Flynn 500," a giant, Japanese-bound book of over five hundred stories from the community. Bishop is a member of the California School Library Association and past president of CSLA's Northern Region. During her tenure, she created a variety of workshops and events for school librarians and produced a school library advocacy video with interviews of famous children's authors stating the importance of school libraries. She is a member of ALA and AASL and has presented workshops at CSLA and during pre-conference sessions at AASL. She is also active in the book arts community and encourages students to write their own stories and enter them into the Ezra Jack Keats Bookmaking Competition, where her students have won many prizes. She is the Teacher Librarian at Aptos Middle School in San Francisco.

Chapter One: Trials & Challenges

Sheryl J. Bize-Boutte is an Oakland writer whose works artfully succeed in getting across deeper meanings about life and the politics of race and economics without breaking out of the narrative, with Oakland often serving as the backdrop for her touching and frequently hilarious short stories. Her first book, *A Dollar Five: Stories from a Baby Boomer's Ongoing Journey* (2014), has been described as "rich in vivid imagery" and "incredible." Her second book, *All That and More's Wedding* (2016), a collection of fictional mystery/crime short stories, is praised as "imaginative with colorful and likeable characters that draw you in to each story and leave you wanting more." Her latest book, *Running for the 2:10* (2017), a follow-on to *A Dollar Five*, delves deeper into her coming of age in Oakland and the embedded issues of race and skin color, with one reviewer calling it "a great contribution to literature."

It has been said that Sheryl "brings down the house" with presentations of her stories and poetry. Her poems "Cutty Sark and Milk (She Said, She Said)" and "Childthink" were winners in the 2019 San Lorenzo Library Literary Contest. You can find more about her work at www.Sjbb-talkinginclass.blogspot.com.
Chapter One: Childhood & Coming of Age

Bea Bowles, a professional storyteller with a passion for stories, was inspired by Spider Grandmother, the creator in Hopi myth and the fairy godmother of Bea's storytelling. Bea weaves webs of tales from different cultures around a shared theme in her live performances, audio storybooks, and her two storybooks, *Spider Secrets* and *Grandmother Spider's Web of Wonders*. Bowles recorded diverse creation stories with Michael and Justine Toms, the pioneering producers of New Dimensions Radio, working with the famous world mythologist, Joseph Campbell. The program, *Children of Desire: Five Creation Stories from Around the World*, is available from New Dimensions and features storytellers from different traditions. Teachers and students give Bea Bowles rave reviews whenever she visits their schools, saying: "One of the loveliest qualities that Beatrice brings to our classroom is an understanding of different world cultures though the stories she tells and weaves together." A producer from Audible Books endorsed her, stating, "With over eight hours of stories to choose from, we elected to start the collection off with one from Beatrice, since she has the perfect voice and performance style to help one get lost in the world of stories." Visit her at www.beatricebowles.com.
Chapter Two: Defining Story

S.G. Browne is a writer of dark comedy and social satire with a supernatural or fantastic edge. He writes about zombies fighting for their civil rights, private detectives born with the

ability to steal luck, and professional guinea pigs who test pharmaceutical drugs and develop unusual superpowers. His published works include the novels *Breathers, Fated, Lucky Bastard, Big Egos*, and *Less Than Hero*, as well as the short story collection *Shooting Monkeys in a Barrel* and the heartwarming holiday novella *I Saw Zombies Eating Santa Claus*. He's also the author of *The Maiden Poodle*, a fairy tale about anthropomorphic cats and dogs suitable for children and adults of all ages. His writing is influenced by Chuck Palahniuk, Christopher Moore, Kurt Vonnegut, and the films of Charlie Kaufman and Wes Anderson, among others. When not writing, he's reading, biking across the Golden Gate Bridge, doing tai chi, binge-watching Netflix, or volunteering at the San Francisco SPCA. He's also an ice cream connoisseur, Guinness aficionado, and a sucker for *It's a Wonderful Life*. You can learn more about his writing at www.sgbrowne.com.
Chapter Two: Personal Branding Story

Simona Carini was born in Perugia, Italy, and is a graduate of the R. Donatelli School of Nursing in Perugia and of the Catholic University of the Sacred Heart in Milan, Italy, as well as of Mills College in Oakland, California. She writes nonfiction and poetry, has been published in various venues, in print and online, and has won awards for her memoirs and food writing. She is a member of the San Francisco Chapter of the Women's National Book Association and of the Redwood Writers Branch of the California Writers Club. Her memoir "The Blue Backpack" was published in the 2015 Redwood Writers' anthology *Journeys* and reprinted in the 2016 California Writers Club *Literary Review*. She lives in Northern California with her husband and works as an academic researcher in medical information science. Her website is simonacarini.com.
Chapter One: Adventure Stories

Marlene Cullen is enthusiastic about encouraging people to write, even those who think they can't. Her series of books, The Write Spot anthologies, features writing that entertains as well as inspires other writers. Every story, vignette, and poem in The Write Spot books include writing prompts motivating readers to become writers. Fulfilling her passion for writing and sharing with others, Marlene has created unique writing environments such as Jumpstart Writing Workshops, where participants often experience transformational changes. Her workshops provide essential elements for successful writing. Marlene is the founder of Writers Forum of Petaluma, a monthly literary event featuring presenters talking about the craft and business of writing. Marlene's award-winning short stories and essays have been published in literary journals, anthologies, and newspapers, including *Tiny Lights*, *Building Bridges*, *More Bridges*, the Redwood Writers anthologies, and The Write Spot anthologies. She is a member of the California Writer's Club. Marlene hosts The Write Spot Blog, a treasure chest of inspirational gems for writers at www. TheWriteSpot.us.

Chapter Three: Family Secrets & Shadows

Sara Etgen-Baker's love for words began when, as a young girl, her mother read the dictionary to her every night. A teacher's unexpected whisper, "You've got writing talent," ignited her writing desire. Although Sara ignored that whisper and pursued a different career, she eventually rediscovered her inner writer. Sara has written over a hundred memoir vignettes and narrative essays, many of which have won awards and been published in e-zines, blogs, anthologies, and magazines, including WomensMemoirs.com, *The Preserve Journal*, *Chicken Soup for the Soul*, *Guideposts*, *Wisdom Has a Voice*, *Table for Two*, *Finding Mr. Right*, *Inside and Out: Women's Truths*, *Women's Stories*, and *Times They Were A-Changing:*

Women Remember the '60s & '70s. Sara's novel-in-progress, *Secrets at Dillehay Crossing*, was a finalist in the 2017 Vinnie Ream Letters contest sponsored by the National League of American Pen Women, of which she is a member. Sara is also a member of Story Circle Network and regularly contributes to its One Woman's Day blog and its quarterly journal. Sara also works with the Anna Area Historical Society in Texas, researching and writing historical documents that preserve Anna's history. When not writing, Sara enjoys walking and spending time with her husband, Bill.
Chapter One: Childhood & Coming of Age

Betsy Graziani Fasbinder is an author, psychotherapist, podcaster, public speaking teacher, and coach. Whether in our intimate conversations, our written stories, or our professional lives, it's her belief that it is in our stories that the deepest connections can be made. She is the host of the Morning Glory Project: Stories of Determination, as well as author of a novel, *Fire & Water*, a memoir, *Filling Her Shoes*, and an instructive nonfiction book, *From Page to Stage: Inspiration, Tools, and Public Speaking Tips for Writers*. To find out more, contact Betsy at www.betsygrazianifasbinder.com.
Chapter Two: Signature Story

Joan Gelfand is the author of *You Can Be a Winning Writer*, a writing coach, and a presenter. She has written three acclaimed volumes of poetry, an award-winning chapbook of short fiction, and *Fear to Shred*, a novel set in a Silicon Valley startup. The recipient of numerous writing awards, commendations, nominations, and honors, Joan's work appears in the *Los Angeles Review of Books*, The Huffington Post, *Rattle, Prairie Schooner, Kalliope, The Meridian Anthology of Contemporary Poetry*, the *Toronto Review, Marsh Hawk Review, Levure Litteraire, Chicken Soup for the*

Soul, and over one hundred anthologies and journals. A film based on Joan's poem, "The Ferlinghetti School of Poetics," was featured at eight international film festivals, including Cannes, Rome, Hollywood, London and Malta. It showed at the Poetry Film Festival in Athens, Greece, and won a Certificate of Merit at the International Association for the Study of Dreams. The poem was crafted from three dreams about Lawrence Ferlinghetti Joan had over the course of a year. Joan is a member of the National Book Critics Circle and Bay Area Travel Writers and a past president of the Women's National Book Association. She is a juror for the Northern California Book Awards. Visit her at joangelfand.com.

Chapter Two: Signature Story

Humaira Ghilzai is a writer, speaker, and consultant on the culture of Afghanistan. Humaira opens the world to Afghan culture and cuisine through her wildly popular blog, Afghan Culture Unveiled. She shares the wonders of Afghanistan through stories of rich culture, delicious food, and her family's traditions. Humaira is a member of Women's National Book Association and is currently working on her first novel, *Unraveling Veils*, which is set in San Francisco and Afghanistan. Humaira's writing has been published in *Encore Magazine, Mataluna: A book of 152 Afghan Pashto Proverbs,* and *Medium*. Her website is www.humairaghilzai.com.

Chapter Three: Family Folklore

Lee Goff is an author, businessman, business owner, husband, father, grandfather, and friend. He is formally educated, having received undergraduate degrees in both English and finance and one graduate degree. Lee is the son of a career military officer; he grew up in a household considered normal at the time with a loving mother and father, then experienced the struggle of coping with a mother in the grips of Alzheimer's

and dementia long before modern medicine and therapy were available to understand and deal with it. The rest of Lee's life has been full of mistakes they call lessons, lessons he tried to turn into wisdom, as well as a faith in God that he sees as his foundation for all things. Visit him at www.thundertrilogy.com.
Chapter One: Trials & Challenges

Claire Hennessy, author and storyteller, moved from the UK to live in California in 2008, the shock of which propelled her to start writing as a form of cheap therapy. She is currently editing her humorous memoir about how she and her husband reunited after not seeing each other for over thirty years. She is hoping to get it published before she is too old to go on a book tour. She is a founding member of Write on Mamas (writeonmamas.com), a San Francisco Bay Area writing group. She has been published in four anthologies, including the Award-winning *She's Got This: Essays on Standing Strong and Moving On* and *Nothing but the Truth So Help Me God— Transitions*. She has performed at Lit Quake, Lit Crawl, The Moth, The Marsh, and other storytelling events and venues. Visit her podcast *The Bonkers Brit*.
Chapter Three: Family Folklore

KJ Landis is an author, educator, and health and life coach. She holds a bachelor of science degree in education and has certificates in personal training, Pilates, and fitness class instruction, as well as certificates in continuing education in psychology, global health, childhood development, and nutrition at Stanford School of Medicine, Johns Hopkins University, and other prestigious universities. Her focus is on teaching a grain-free and sugar-free lifestyle, deciphering food labels, and instructing individuals on how to build a tribe of support when making any lifestyle change for the better. Landis consults with clients locally in San Francisco and remotely, via internet and phone, as far as Dubai. She has created and facilitates wellness workshops in libraries, senior centers, for corporations, and in private homes. KJ Landis has been a featured guest on the *HCG Body for Life* podcast, *Newbie Writers* podcast, and more. She has written numerous books on wellness. Her weekly videos and blogs share information on holistic health topics as well as providing motivational and inspirational support. You may read more about KJ Landis and her personal journey to wellness at www. superiorselfwithkjlandis.com.

Chapter Three: Family Secrets & Shadows

Jing Li is originally from China. Her soon to be published memoir, *The Red Sandals*, is a coming-of-age survival story in a country that devalues female infants. Her mother tried to terminate her pregnancy while pregnant with Jing, then abandoned her; she was raised by her paternal, peasant grandmother, who was inclined toward infanticide of female babies and had no use for girls. Later, when Jing herself gave birth to a girl, her father-in-law pressured her to have her infant daughter lethally injected. Jing is a member of the California Writers Club (CWC) and Women's National Book Association, San Francisco Chapter. Her personal narratives have won awards: the Grand Prize in the 2017 San Francisco Writing Contest sponsored by the San Francisco Writers Conference ("The Red Sandals"); First Place, CWC, Redwood Branch Memoir Contest 2015 ("My First Watermelon"); the True Grit Award/Mt. Hermon Writers Conference, 2014 ("My Surviving Life Story in China"); and Second Place in CWC's Jack London Writers Contest, Nonfiction, 2007 ("My Story as a New American Immigrant"). Jing's personal stories have been published in *California Writers Club Literary Magazine*, 2019, 2018; *The Magic of Memoir*, She Writes Press, 2016; *Healdsburg and Beyond!* A Healdsburg Literary Guild Book,

2016; *Untold Stories: From the Deep Part of the Well*, CWC Redwood Writers Anthology, 2016; *Journeys on the Road & Off the Map*, Redwood Writers Anthology, 2015; and *Water*, CWC Redwood Writers Anthology, 2014. Visit her at JingLiTheRedSandals.com.
Chapter One: Childhood & Coming of Age

Mary Mackey became a writer by running high fevers, tramping through tropical jungles, dodging machine-gun fire, being caught in volcanic eruptions, swarmed by army ants, stalked by vampire bats, threatened by poisonous snakes, making catastrophic decisions about men, and reading. She is the author of fourteen novels including The *Village of Bones* and *The Year the Horses Came*, which describe how the peaceful Goddess-worshiping people of Prehistoric Europe fought off patriarchal nomad invaders. Mary's novels have made *The New York Times* and *San Francisco Chronicle* bestseller lists, have been translated into twelve foreign languages, and have sold over a million and a half copies. Mary is also the author of eight collections of poetry including *The Jaguars That Prowl Our Dreams*, winner of the 2019 Erich Hoffer Award for the Best Book Published by a Small Press and a 2018 Women's Spirituality Book Award; and *Sugar Zone*, winner of the 2012 PEN Oakland Josephine Miles Award. Often set in the jungles of the Brazilian Amazon, her poems have been praised by Maxine Hong Kingston, Wendell Berry, Jane Hirshfield, D. Nurkse, Al Young, and Marge Piercy for their beauty, precision, originality, and extraordinary range. Visit her website at marymackey.com.
Chapter One: Adventure Stories

Marissa Moss, award-winning children's author and illustrator, has produced several popular picture books, as well as a series of beginning readers featuring a young writer named

Amelia. Beginning with *Amelia's Notebook*, Marissa follows her eponymous heroine through a series of daily adventures in the fourth grade: The young protagonist changes schools, makes new friends, and copes with an annoying older sister. Marissa has also written several historical journals, also in diary format, such as the Young American Voices series, among them *Emma's Journal: The Story of a Colonial Girl*, *Hannah's Journal: The Story of an Immigrant Girl*, and *Rose's Journal: The Story of a Girl in the Great Depression*. Marissa's keen interest in history and her passion to share notable events in history with children has prompted her to continue to produce award-winning picture books, such as *Barb Wired Baseball* and *The Eye That Never Sleeps: How Detective Pinkerton Saved President Lincoln*. A departure and unique publication, *Last Things: A Graphic Memoir of Loss and Love*, is an illustrated story for adults. It is deeply personal and tells of the loss of Marissa's husband—how a family managed to survive a terrible loss and grow in spite of it. Visit her at marrissamoss.com.

Chapter Two: Personal Branding Story

Linda Joy Myers, author of the award-winning memoir *Song of the Plains*, grew up in Enid, Oklahoma, where she experienced the power and beauty of the landscape and the people who marked her soul for life. In her writing, she seeks to explore the themes of healing abandonment, secrets, and silence. Her memories of the wind, the land, and her family weave together to show the power of memory and personal history. Her first memoir, *Don't Call Me Mother*, is about healing three generations of mother-daughter abandonment. Linda Joy is the president and founder of the National Association of Memoir Writers. Linda has been a therapist for the last forty years and enjoys coaching writers who are capturing the stories that have stayed too long in silence.

Linda is the author of *The Power of Memoir* and *Journey of Memoir*, and coauthor of *Breaking Ground on Your Memoir* and *The Magic of Memoir*. Please visit her at: www.lindajoymyersauthor.com and www.namw.org.

Chapter Two: Defining Story

Beverly Scott was curious about her mysterious grandfather for many years while she pursued her career and raised a daughter. After her career as an organization consultant and leadership coach began to wind down, she launched a genealogy journey to uncover the secrets her grandmother had never revealed. Although she discovered the rumors about her grandfather were true, there were many missing pieces of the story. Bev decided to use what she had learned as a foundation to write a historical novel, *Sarah's Secret: A Western Tale of Betrayal and Forgiveness*. In addition to her thirty-seven-year consulting career, Bev served as the executive director for a community action agency during the "War on Poverty" and taught sociology to undergraduates at both Cornell College and Coe College in Iowa and in the Organization Psychology Master's program at John F. Kennedy University in the San Francisco Bay Area. She has written many professional articles and published three books, the latest of which was coauthored with Kim Barnes and published in 2011, *Consulting on the Inside*. She has served as chair of the board of the Horizon Foundation, the Organization Development Network, and the Women's Justice Center. More information is available on her website www.bevscott.com.

Chapter Three: Family Legacy Stories

Waights Taylor Jr. was born and raised in Birmingham, Alabama, and has written five books, starting with two nonfiction books: *Alfons Mucha's Slav Epic: An Artist's History of the Slavic People* (2008), and the award-winning *Our Southern Home: Scottsboro to Montgomery to Birmingham—The Transformation of the South in the Twentieth Century* (2011). An award-winning murder mystery trilogy followed, featuring private detectives Joe McGrath and Sam Rucker: *Kiss of Salvation* (2014), *Touch of Redemption* (2016), and concluding the trilogy, *Heed the Apocalypse* (2017). Taylor's next book is the soon to be published young adult novel, *Henry Tuttle—The Boy Who Loved to Run*. Taylor now lives in Santa Rosa, California, with his wife, Elizabeth Martin, surrounded by five wonderful children and seven terrific grandchildren.

Chapter Three: Family Legacy Stories

Michel Wing identifies as a nonbinary, disabled writer, living and working in New Mexico. They have spent the bulk of their life working on visibility and issues such as domestic violence awareness, disability rights, sexual assault prevention, and LGBTQI advocacy. Their publications include *Body on the Wall* (poems) and *Cry of the Nightbird: Writers Speak Against Domestic Violence* (as coeditor), both under the name of Michelle Wing. Michel's narrative pieces, including a few showing their more humorous side, have recently been published in *The Write Spot: Reflections*, edited by Marlene Cullen. Their poetry and essays have also been anthologized widely. In addition to writing, Michel ran a five-year program with the YWCA called Changing Hurt to Hope, encouraging others to write and then speak out on the theme of domestic violence. They also started a reading series, "Books on Stage," which continues to this day. Both of these were in Sonoma County, California. In New Mexico, as a guest artist, they facilitated the creation of a chapbook with Young Women United on the theme of issues around pregnancy and access to services for Latina women. Michel blogs about life with a service dog at www.caninebodhisattva.com.

Chapter One: Trials & Challenges

Acknowledgements

This book would not exist without the gentle insistence of Alex Fischer, who prompted me to find a book I'd lost, one I'd written in 1979: *Word Weaving: A Storytelling Workbook*, published by the Zellerbach Family Fund, San Francisco. Once this first storytelling book was found, my librarian colleagues, in particular Lisa Bishop, urged me to update the book with new storytelling content and purpose. With the wonderful and persistent support of Brenda Knight, associate publisher at Mango Publishing, Inc., I was able to prepare a successful book proposal and begin the writing process. I am greatly indebted to the twenty-one expert contributors to the book who shared their compelling stories and storytelling tips, ensuring that this book included diverse voices and styles. And to all my friends in the writing and storytelling community, I am grateful for your collaboration and for the many opportunities to publish over the years—as I evolved in my understanding of the power of personal narrative. Finally, thanks to my son, Brendan Farrell, who listened to my stories from the very beginning and still does.

About the Author

Kate Farrell believes in the power of story. A graduate of the School of Library and Information Studies, UC Berkeley, she has been a language arts classroom teacher (preschool and grades kindergarten through twelfth), author, librarian, university lecturer, and storyteller in Northern California since 1966. Kate founded the Word Weaving Storytelling Project in collaboration with the California State Department of Education, funded by grants from the Zellerbach Family Fund, San Francisco, 1979–1991, to train educators at all levels, and published numerous educational materials.

Kate is coauthor of a monograph, *Word Weaving: A Storytelling Workbook*, 1980 and *Effects of Storytelling: An Ancient Art for Modern Classrooms*, 1982. She is the author of

Word Weaving: A Teaching Sourcebook, 1984 and producer and coauthor of a training videotape, "Word Weaving: The Art of Storytelling," 1983, distributed by the University of California, Berkeley. She is also the author of the professional book, *Storytelling: A Guide for Teachers*, Scholastic, 1991. She is senior author of *Storytelling in Our Multicultural World*, an oral language development program for early childhood education published by Zaner-Bloser, Educational Publishers of Highlights for Children, 1994.

Recently, Kate's stories have appeared in numerous anthologies, and she edited an anthology of personal narrative, *Wisdom Has a Voice: Every Daughter's Memories of Mother*. She is the coeditor of the award-winning anthologies, *Times They Were A-Changing: Women Remember the '60s & '70s*, and *Cry of the Nightbird: Writers Against Domestic Violence*.

Mango Publishing, established in 2014, publishes an eclectic list of books by diverse authors—both new and established voices—on topics ranging from business, personal growth, women's empowerment, LGBTQ studies, health, and spirituality to history, popular culture, time management, decluttering, lifestyle, mental wellness, aging, and sustainable living. We were recently named 2019's #1 fastest growing independent publisher by *Publishers Weekly*. Our success is driven by our main goal, which is to publish high quality books that will entertain readers as well as make a positive difference in their lives.

Our readers are our most important resource; we value your input, suggestions, and ideas. We'd love to hear from you—after all, we are publishing books for you!

Please stay in touch with us and follow us at:

Facebook: Mango Publishing

Twitter: @MangoPublishing

Instagram: @MangoPublishing

LinkedIn: Mango Publishing

Pinterest: Mango Publishing

Sign up for our newsletter at www.mangopublishinggroup.com and receive a free book!

Join us on Mango's journey to reinvent publishing, one book at a time.

CPSIA information can be obtained
at www.ICGtesting.com
Printed in the USA
BVHW032028300920
590032BV00003B/3